Over the River:

My Journey Home

James Melvin Proctor

ISBN 978-1-7320008-9-6

Library of Congress Control Number 2018 965271

Published by

merge
Publishing Group, LLC

Emerge Publishing Group, LLC
Riviera Beach, FL
www.emergepublishers.com

James Melvin Proctor 2018
Over the River: My Journey Home

Printed in the United States of America

Contents

DEDICATION

---◆---

I dedicate this book to my wife Rose whose love and devotion never wavered. Her quiet, steady, unfailing support has been a source of strength for more than six decades.

James M. Proctor

FOREWORD

---◆---

Dr. James Proctor's journey, "Over the River," has deep roots in the Judeo-Christian tradition. It harkens back to the Hebrews' 40 years of tribulations in the desert followed by the crossing over the Jordan River to the Promised Land. It also brings to mind Jesus' "Over the River" journey, particularly his agonizing struggles in the Garden of Gethsemane, abandonment by the disciples and ultimately, death on the cross and resurrection. James Proctor was born in 1929 near the Florida-Georgia border. As a Black youth, he confronted the harsh realities of racial prejudice, including segregation, low income and limited educational opportunities, as well as skepticism from family relatives and classmates about his capacity to overcome these obstacles.

Unlike many persons faced with similar hardships, James Proctor was determined to meet these challenges with unswerving dedication, hard work, humility and temperance. He refused to succumb to resentment or resignation, seeking instead the higher ground of faith, hope and charity. Raised in the African Methodist Episcopal (AME) Church, he embraced the key tenets of his denomination's Book of

Discipline and the commandment Jesus gave to the Apostle Peter three times, "Feed my sheep!"

Over the past 66 years, he has done just that. He has served as sergeant in the U.S. Army, public high school teacher in vocational agriculture, Associate Executive Director of the New York State Council of Churches focusing on the needs of migrant workers, Florida State University Assistant Professor of Social Work, AME pastor and presiding elder, and core member of the African-American Alzheimer's Caregiver Training and Support (ACTS) Project.

James Proctor is my mentor and close, personal friend. Over the past 12 years he has guided me in developing and implementing ACTS to distressed African-American caregivers of older adults with dementia across North and Central Florida. James' integrity, fervor for social justice and health equity, and commitment to service has moved me profoundly. He is my role model and spiritual father. I know you will find Dr. Proctor's memoir as compelling as I have found my personal faith journey with him.

Robert L. Glueckauf, Ph. D., Professor
College of Medicine Florida State University

PREFACE

As I get older, I sense in unique ways the end of life is nearing. I sense this by the gradual decline in health and the frequent reminders of the demise of relatives, friends, professional associates and acquaintances. There is also the reminder of increased physician visits, more pains, less energy and the inability to do and enjoy many of the things I once enjoyed. It was these types of reminders that prompted me to write this book. I want to share some of my experiences, struggles, and accomplishments with members of my family, especially my grands and great grandchildren, other relatives, friends, men and women with whom I work in the Justice Ministry, the African American Alzheimer's Training and Support Project, ministerial colleagues who are actively engaged in ministry, those I am mentoring, and those who frequently seek my advice and counsel. I hope this book will give them courage to fight the good fight and never give up.

This book contains some of the memorable times in my life. It is a recollection of struggles and triumphs, of failures and successes. It is, for me, a time of looking back as if from a distance. It is a time of reflection, recalling, reliving some dark times, and enjoying those times of light and successes. The book is a recognition, by the help of God, I made it "over the river" and made significant contributions.

These high moments in my life are divided into four specific types. One type I call spiritual accomplishments, or spiritual highs. Among those times were: 1) my conversion experience, the time when I accepted Jesus Christ as Lord and Savior; 2) the time I acknowledged the call to preach the gospel; 3) the ordination as an Itinerant Elder in the African Methodist Episcopal Church; and 4) the time I led the people of God at Saint Paul A. M. E. Church from an obsolete facility in the urban core section of Jacksonville, Florida to a major highway and constructed one of denomination's finest worship and community facility.

The second type of accomplishments are related to educational attainment: a) the first African American male to graduate from high school in east rural Jefferson County Florida, b) first in my family to graduate from college, c) the earning of a Master of Divinity, Master of Social Work and a Doctor of Ministry degree from Drew University. These were all high moments in my life. A third type of highs were professional positions. I will summarize them in these categories: 1) teaching at the high school, college and university levels, 2) director of the mental health services at Jordan Health Center, Rochester, New York, 3) my vocation as a minister of the gospel of Jesus Christ as a community development worker with the New York State Council of Churches, 4) as pastor in the African Methodist Episcopal Church. This book contains some highs and lows from each of these experiences.

It is my hope you journey with me and experience my struggles and my achievements. It is not my intent to share every detail of my life. However, I want you to feel some of the pains, the challenges and the disappointments. I also want you to experience with me, the highs, the sense of accomplishments, the sense of crossing the river. I invite you to travel with me from the stinging days of segregation, through Jim crow, and separate but equal, desegregation, to a period in our national life when we have a Chief divider as head of our national government. I invite you, in the words of the Hebrew Scriptures *"Let justice roll down like waters, and righteousness like an ever-flowing stream" (Amos 5:24 NRSV).*

CHAPTER 1

EARLY YEARS

---◆---

My Parents

The voyage of life for James Melvin Proctor began on a cool Friday evening, September 13, 1929 at approximately 8:30 o'clock in a rural community near Ashville, Florida. James, the first born of four siblings, began his journey of upward mobility that took him to unimaginable heights. His parents were energetic, hard-working, ordinary people who set high standards for themselves and their children. His father, James Alfred Proctor was witty, eager to learn, with excellent leadership skills. James' mother was ingénues, thrifty, feisty, and deeply spiritual. By the time he was six years old his parents had moved three times, trying to make life better for this young family. It was at this time, life around James began to take on meaning.

We were now living in a four-room, recently constructed frame house. Our home was located on the Gerald Livingston Plantation, approximately four miles east of the Aucilla River. My paternal grandparents lived approximately a mile south of us on another farm, across an unnamed stream of water. To visit our paternal grandparents, we would cross the stream on logs, elevated above the water. Although my paternal grandparents were closer in proximity; they seemed distant, cold, unwelcoming, and uninviting. They were not the grandparents I was eager to visit.

On the other hand, my maternal grandparents lived seven or eight miles away, west of the Aucilla River. A visit to their home was always welcoming, invigorating, uplifting, reassuring, nurturing and filled with warmth and love. When my siblings and I went "over the river" to our maternal grandparent's home, we were made to feel special. We listened to our grandparent's stories about their economic struggles, the oppressive racial issues and bigoted law enforcement officers. The days and weeks spent at our maternal grandparents' home were educationally stimulating and filled with excitement!

Our great grandmother, Elizabeth Sneed would keep me spellbound. She talked about the "Emancipation Proclamation." She told us, when the president decided to "free the slaves, it was a happy day of jubilation." Grand Ma Liz's stories of struggle, hard work, hardship and survival were vivid word pictures of overcoming. Therefore, "over the river" took on a special meaning for me at an early age. "Over the river" meant hugs and genuine displays of love, affection, affirmation and acceptance from extended family members. "Over the river" also meant being nurtured and reassured by people outside of my immediate family.

Visiting my maternal great grandparents reinforced my parents' message that my destiny was not determined by my present state, nor past circumstances. "Over the river" was a link to the past but it always pointed upward. I knew I was meant to go up the social economic ladder. It meant, I had to acquire an education, skills and a good job to make life better for me and for others.

The Aucilla River was more than a physical barrier that separated one section of Jefferson County from the other. The river separated families, traditions and cultures. At times, there was tension between some families who lived west of the Aucilla River and those who lived on the east side, as we did. Some of that tension gradually faded away during my generation. This was due, in part, to men and women on one side of the river marrying people who lived on the other side and raising families. Also, it was due to high school students meeting and studying together in the one African American High School in the county, at that time.

My father, like other men in the community his age, was a share cropper. Share cropping was a fiscal disaster for tenants. The plantation owners always were the winners and the share croppers were always the losers. I remember my father saying to my mother, one evening, around the fireplace, six or seven days before Christmas, "Today was check-up time." There was a long pause before dad continued. Then he said, "Things may be rough next year, but I'll never sharecrop another day in my life." Dad went on to say, "As much cotton as we grew and all the corn we harvested, plus the watermelons and peanuts we sold, I don't have enough money to buy Santa Claus for these children." To which mom responded, "The Lord will see us through."

At six years of age, I did not understand the full meaning of "check-up time." I later learned that the plantation owner kept the records of what was provided to the tenants during the year for planting, cultivating and harvesting the crops. The owner also kept the records on how much was harvested. The land owner always cheated the tenants, and their crops never produced enough to completely pay off the land owner. It was a system of economic exploitation and deprivation on a grand scale.

I do not remember what my three siblings and I received for Christmas that year. I do recall the first Saturday in January, dad left home walking about eight o'clock on a frigid, cold morning and returned in a new one-horse wagon with a gold color guernsey heifer tied to the wagon. When we saw the wagon coming from a distance, we went outside to wave as it passed by. But as it got closer we recognized that it was dad. We all ran down the road, meeting dad and riding the last few hundred yards. A few weeks later this young female cow gave birth to a calf and we were blessed with approximately six to eight quarts of rich, fresh milk twice a day. Immediately we were recognized by our neighbors as on the rise. It was not very long before everyone in the neighborhood knew the Proctor family had milk and butter, and they would share it.

My dad was no longer a sharecropper. He was now an entrepreneur, renting land from the plantation owner and paying a specified amount at the end of the harvest season. Dad now kept his own records of how much money he borrowed from the bank to purchase seed, fertilizers etc. to plant and produce crops. God blessed dad's fields and the harvest was plentiful. Dad was able to pay for the mule, wagon and the cow, plus the rent with money left. Mom and dad were pleased the way this venture succeeded at the end of the first year. From that small but adventurous step, bigger things happened. By the end of the third year, dad owned four mules, a two-horse wagon, cultivators, a truck, cows, hogs, goats and other farm animals.

With the beginning of the Second World War on December 7, 1941, the price of farm produce nearly tripled. Dad increased the acreage under cultivation, raised hogs for market, and our economic standing was not nearly as bleak as three years earlier. I do not intend to imply that we had moved into the middle class, far from it. I simply mean our parents were setting examples for their children and others in the community to use one's God-given abilities to improve one's position in life.

At six years old I was enrolled in elementary school. My first three years of schooling was spent at Antioch African Methodist Episcopal Church, on County Road 146, Ashville Highway. There were approximately thirty students in that one room, taught by a dedicated, but not formerly educated teacher. By fourth grade the county had built a two-room school and two teachers who were graduates of Florida A and M College were assigned as our teachers. Mr. Walden, my fourth-grade teacher, made learning fun and exciting. He taught grades four through eight. I was thrilled to be in his classes and hated to miss any days from school.

With the war raging, most able-bodied young men were drafted for military service. Others left the farm for higher paying industrial jobs in large metropolitan areas. Dad was unable to hire laborers to help with the farm work, so at the age of twelve I became a dependable farm worker. Many days, instead of attending school, I was working alongside my dad, tilling the soil, planting, cultivating and harvesting the crops. It was hard work, but it taught me valuable lessons. The two or three days I attended school each week helped me appreciate learning. At home I read whatever magazines and newspapers were available and each evening, I had to tell my parents and siblings at least one thing I learned that day. This was our parent's way of re-enforcing the importance of education. It taught me to be observant of my surroundings, and it gave me the ability to express myself. The days I was able to attend class, I was able to finish my assignments in a very short time and the teacher allowed me to help the other students. This gave me confidence and made me feel special. Despite the absences during the planting and growing seasons, I graduated Valedictorian of my eighth-grade class.

As I matriculated through elementary school the teachings of my parents began to take root in my life. The daily Scripture reading, and memorization became a ritual that took on deep spiritual meaning. To witness my father and mother kneeling beside our beds and praying each morning made an indelible imprint on me. Dad would often use the words of hymns to convey his message to God and to me. One such hymn was written by Isaac Watts:

"O that I knew the secret place where I might mind my God!
I'd spread my wants before His face and pour my woes abroad.

My God will pity my complaints, and heal my broken bones;
He takes the meaning of His saints, the language of their groans.

Arise, my soul, from deep distress, and banish every fear; He
calls thee His throne of grace, to spread thy sorrows there."

(338 AMECH)

At other times dad would pray: "O Lord, bless our children. They are the off springs of our bodies. Help us to raise them up in thy fear that they may learn early to serve and glorify your holy name."

We were taught, more than taught, we were indoctrinated that one had to admit that one was a sinner, believe in one's heart that Jesus died for me, and confess Jesus Christ as Lord and Savior. This was called a conversion experience. At the age of twelve I experienced this unique, indiscernible reality. It was a life changing experience. It was an out of this world experience. I felt the overpowering presence of the Holy Spirit. I felt a new source of the presence of God in my life. I told my parents and everyone I encountered that God for Christ's sake had forgiven me of my sins and I had committed my life to him. From that day until now that initial encounter with God has been an empowering, centering, spiritual force in my life. This encounter was indeed a high moment I hope you experience with me. There have been times I have failed in my commitment to the risen Christ, but I have soon found my way back to his presence.

It is that faith that has guided me and helped me to overcome tremendous odds and achieve beyond my wildness imagination.

Although, I have tried to live a life before my son and grandsons that reflect a spiritual anchor, I admit I was not as deliberate as was my father. My son has often heard me pray and preach and teach. He has often seen the role I have played to advance the cause of justice and stand against injustices in secular and religious enterprises. My son has observed the sacrifices I have made to mentor others, sometimes at great cost to my family and myself.

CHAPTER 2

HIGH SCHOOL YEARS

———◆———

There was only one high school in the county that African American children could attend. That high school, Howard Academy, was thirteen miles from where I lived. Again, I lived east of the Aucilla River. To attend High School in

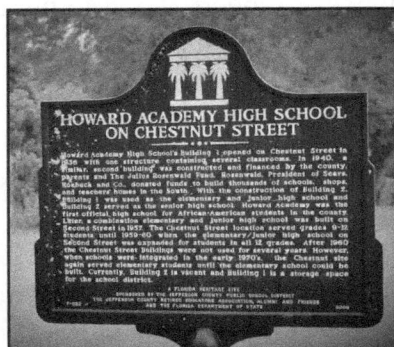

Howard Academy Sign

Monticello meant crossing the river; and Jefferson Country Public School System did not provide transportation for its black students.

My parents arranged for me to live with a public-school teacher's family in Monticello from Sunday evening until Friday afternoon. That period of my life took on a new dimension. I had to adjust to a new family structure and values. I felt lost for the first few days, getting out of school at 3:00 o'clock in the afternoon and no farm animals to feed and water, no wood to cut or the hundred other things to do on a farm. I soon discovered, however, the family with whom I lived raised hogs on the outskirts of town. I joined my landlord in tending the hogs; and got a job at the United States Post Office, cleaning the floors and delivering Special Delivery mail. On some Friday evenings I would go home to live with my parents and other siblings, and to do whatever work there was to be done on the farm. There was always an abundance of work to do. There was the ground to till, crops to plant, cultivate, harvest and market; animals to tend, fences to mend, wood to cut and on and on. There was never a dull moment on the farm.

In Monticello, each day I attended classes and came home and volunteered to help with the chores. The family with whom I lived during the week was very pleased with my industrious skills. After the first few weeks, I was informed that I would not be charged for living with them. I was treated as a member of the family. They shared their food, gave encouraging words and treated me as if I were a member of the family.

I did exceptionally well in school. I had a perfect attendance record, was never late and was always courteous and polite to all the teachers. I also became very popular with both boys and girls in my High School classes. This was true because I often helped them with homework assignments and research papers. On the other hand, some of my peers in High School said negative things, such as, "Here comes plow boy. Ask him, he knows the answer;" just loud enough that I could hear them. Moreover, when I went home on the weekends, boys in the community where I grew up, made fun at me; calling me names, saying "there's that 'sissy' who attends fancy schools." It was not called bullying then. But it was devastating and humiliating. I could never physically win a fight. Most of the boys were stronger than I. My only weapon, I thought, was to act as if I did not hear those comments and continued to study and be friendly to everyone, hoping this would win them to my side. I was not deterred, I studied harder, expressed myself fluently and became increasingly active in church.

As I progressed academically, I also grew spiritually. From my childhood my parents often read the Scriptures and prayed aloud at their children's bedside. My dad often prayed, "O God, bless these children, the off-springs of our bodies. Help us to raise them up in thy fear that they may learn early, to serve and glorify your holy name."

During my high school year, I was given increased responsibilities in the rural church I attended with family and other residents of the community. While I was still in High School, the pastor of our local African Methodist Episcopal church appointed me to serve as superintendent of the Sunday school. Among my responsibilities were to lead and facilitate the Sunday's school each Sunday, help select teachers for each class and make reports to the church's Official Board about the progress of the Sunday school. This training was invaluable. It gave me hands-on leadership experience at an early age. I learned how to set goals, plan, organize and work with others, most times; I worked with people much older than myself.

About midway through my freshman year in high school, I learned that many of my dad's peers, other farmers, even dad's brother tried to discourage my parents from sending me to school. On one occasion just before school began for my sophomore year, I overheard my dad and my uncle, dad's brother, engaged in a heated argument.

Dad's brother said, "You are wasting money sending that boy to school."

Dad replied, "It is my money, and I have not asked your advice."

Others in the community would talk about our parents, saying, "They think their children are better than the rest of the children; that is why they are sending them to school." It was the custom in the community to educate the daughters in the family, not the sons. Boys in the community bought in to this idea and whenever they saw me, they called me names as identified above. These views expressed by some members of our community were articulated by the white plantation owners whose children were attending school every day. The plantation owners knew, if they kept the black males from getting an education, they would always have an adequate supply of cheap labor.

The weekends at home were difficult days for me. Even as a teenager, I thought a community was about encouraging, nurturing and empowering its youth rather than discouraging them. Each weekend, I went home, I heard snickering and whispers from boys in my age group saying mean things. During the week, when I was in school I heard both good and bad comments. The comments from teachers were always reassuring and encouraging. They helped me to gain confidence and boosted by desire to strive higher and higher. On the other hand, some students were envious of my skills and called me "plow boy" because I lived on a farm, and my clothes were not as fancy as theirs.

High School for me, in some ways, was a period of rapid social adjustment. I had to learn to live away from my immediate family, adjust to the customs of a surrogate family, endure the feeling of being an outsider, and succeed academically. All these experiences however, enriched my life and served to make me more determined to excel.

On June 3, 1949, I graduated salutatorian of my High School class, and was voted, by my classmates as "most likely to succeed." High School graduation was a big day for my family and me. It meant that I had succeeded against the odds. High School graduation meant that I had made my parents proud. I had proved the naysayers wrong. It meant, I became the first African American male from the Ashville community, "over the river" to graduate from High School. My dad was beaming with joy when my name was called to receive my diploma. He marveled at the gifts, congratulatory messages, money and the wonderful things strangers said to him about his son. This was a special night for my dad for another reason. I had proven his distractors wrong. My dad could proudly look his peers in the eyes and boast of his son's accomplishment, despite great difficulty.

June 3, 1949 was special for another reason. My mother was discharged from a hospital with what was, at that time, major surgery. Mom was too weak from the surgery and the hospital stay to attend my graduation. Yet, her face blazed with unspeakable joy and excitement when I reached her bedside with my diploma in one hand and numerous gifts, cards, messages, etc. in the other hand. There were smiles on everyone faces and my mom said in a low but excited voice, "We made liars out of the skeptics. I knew you could do it!"

CHAPTER 3

COLLEGE, EARLY DAYS

———◆———

A week or two after high school graduation, I received my acceptance letter to attend Florida Agricultural and Mechanical University, Tallahassee, FL. I worked extremely hard on the farm all summer trying to earn enough money to purchase school clothes, dormitory necessities, make deposit for ROTC uniforms, and pay tuition. At the end of the summer I discovered that was more money than I could earn. What I realized, September was not market time for most of the crops we were producing. Therefore, it was difficult to acquire $125.25 to enter college in 1949.

I had been an outstanding student in high school, and had received a letter from Sears Roebuck and Company congratulating me on being selected to receive a five hundred-dollar ($500.00) scholarship to major in Agriculture Education. But when I arrived on campus, it took two days to schedule an appointment with the dean of the School of Agriculture.

When I asked Dean Walker, "when would I receive the scholarship?" There was a look of surprise with a response, "What Scholarship?" When I presented the letter, the dean excused himself and went into an adjacent office and called someone on the phone. This lasted for what seemed like an eternity. Finally, the dean returned and said that a mistake had been made.

The scholarship had been awarded to another entering freshman. With that news, I did not have enough money to register for classes. I immediately took a city bus to the greyhound bus station, purchased a roundtrip ticket to Monticello to secure enough money to enroll in college. We lived thirteen miles from the town. When I got off the bus, I started walking the unpaved County Road 146 to my home. I arrived home just as the sun was setting in the western skies.

My mom was the first to see me and yelled, "What's wrong, why did you come back?"

When every one was seated at the kitchen table, one place of physical and emotional nurture, I explained what had happened. In short, I said the five-hundred-dollar scholarship was awarded to another student.

After a few minutes of conversation my mom said, "I think we can find enough money for you to register."

Dad chipped in and asked, "Did your uncle Ernest (his brother), pay you for working the last two weeks?"

My reply was a short, "No sir."

Dad instructed me to go to bed, get a good night's sleep, get up early tomorrow morning, go to my uncle's house and ask him to drive me to the bus station. This would remind him to pay me. that way I would have a little extra money. Although, I had only been gone for three days, and had not attended one class, my siblings asked several questions; such as: How many people go to your college? Do you have any friends? Will you come home every weekend? After dinner, a good bath and following dad's instructions, I was off to bed.

Early the next morning I arrived at my uncle's house before he was out of bed. I called and asked if he would drive me to the bus station. He began to ask several questions: "Why do you need to go to the bus station? Why are you going to Tallahassee so early in the day?" When I replied that I was enrolling in college. He went off in a tirade, saying, "Your daddy needs to keep you here to help him with the farm. That is a waste of money." I had heard that statement before.

All this time, I was standing outside on the porch. Finally, his wife said in a commanding voice, "Get up, take that boy to the bus station. If you would have paid him for working this summer, he would have had enough money." There was silence for a few minutes, then I heard movement coming from inside. He came out and drove me to the bus station, finding fault all the way.

The short thirty-five-minute greyhound bus ride passed quickly, and I was able to register for classes. About midway through the first semester, I learned the dean's fraternity brother's son received the five-hundred-dollar Sears Roebuck and Company scholarship that was intended for me.

For me to matriculate in college, I worked in the dish washing section of the student dining room to pay my tuition. The work was hard; however, I had worked hard all my life. The hours were long, and I had to schedule classes around work time. The scheduled time for work was 7:00 a. m.-8:55 a. m.; 11:00 a. m.-1:55 p. m. and 5:00 p. m. until you finished. Most days I worked 8 hours to pay for tuition, room and board. I made friends with everyone in my work section; this irritated the shift foreman, a school drop-out working in the Florida A and M University dining room. He told the dining room manager that I was "flirting with the women." Immediately, I was called to the office and when I tried to explain my side of the issue I was told "If boss man said you were flirting, you were flirting." With those words I was terminated, one month before the end of my freshman year at the University.

This termination from work meant no money for tuition, room, board, fees, clothing and all the other expenses associated with college. I did not give up. I worked at a dry-cleaning establishment my sophomore year. I was paid a commission for all the clothes I picked up on campus. There were weeks when this job provided substantial income. But there were weeks when I would give credit to my customers who never paid. I had to pay the cost for the cleaning.

If I did not collect the money, I was instructed to return the clothes to the plant. I was too kind for that job. So, at the end of the second year in college, another failure. Grades plummeted, and I was out of college. I did not return home. I could not face the whispers, innuendos and outright ridicule of what would be said about my failure. So, that summer, I hired on as carpenter's helper with a bridge construction company. Ironically, one of the first bridges on which I worked was building the bridge over the Aucilla River on County Road 146 approximately ten miles east of Monticello.

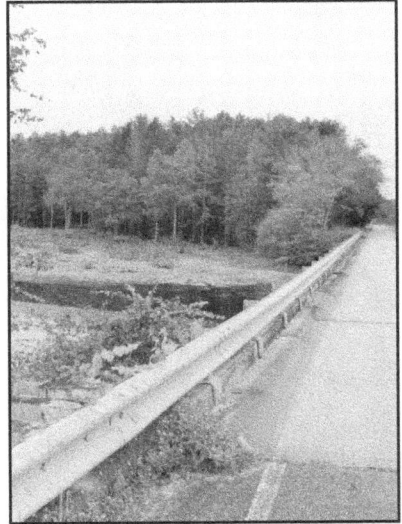

Bridge over the Aucilla River on County Road 146

Two months prior to starting what should have been my junior year in college, I was drafted into the United States Army. The Korean War was raging, and I was one of the more than 5,000,000 men and women who participated in that war. According to http://www.history.com/this-day-in-history/korea. There were approximately 55,000 American casualties.

OVER THE RIVER: MY JOURNEY HOME

CHAPTER 4

OVER THE RIVER WITH THE UNITED STATES ARMY

———◆———

February 12, 1952, began two years of active duty military service in the United States Army. This was the first time I had lived and worked in a diverse, racially integrated environment. The military experience began formerly when approximately fifty other men and I from Alabama, Florida, Louisiana, and Mississippi raised our right hands together and took an oath to defend the Constitution of the United States of America. We became soldiers in the United States Army. The oath is serious business. It reads:

"I, James Melvin Proctor, do solemnly swear (or affirm) that I will support and defend the Constitution of the United States against all enemies, foreign and domestic; that I will bear true faith and allegiance to the same; and that I will obey the orders of the President of the United States and the orders of the officers appointed over me, according to regulations and the Uniform Code of Military Justice. So, help me God."

After the induction ceremony, the recruits were rushed on to railway sleeping cars and awakened the next morning at the 3rd Army

Headquarters, Fort Jackson, South Carolina. Simultaneously, the lights came on, a whistle blew, and standing before us was an overweight, overzealous, neatly attired Army Master Sargent with hash marks a third way up his sleeve, barking out orders. He shouted, "When I call your name, I don't give a damn, who you are, where you are from or what color you are. I want you to say, 'Here Sir' and fall in line."

With those instruction black and white young men from the states of Alabama, Arkansas, Delaware, District of Columbia, Florida, Georgia, Kentucky, Louisiana, Maryland, Mississippi, North Carolina, South Carolina Tennessee, Texas, Virginia, and West Virginia were assigned sleeping quarters in barracks in alphabetical order.

We marched in squads, based on height. These raw recruits soon learned it was never about the individual self. It was always about the success of the unit, the squad, platoon, company, battalion, etc. The first seven to ten days were living hell. Soldiers were marching, eating, sleeping and training next to others who you distrusted because of skin color, and what you had experienced earlier in segregated, oppressive environments. Now, we were told, your very survival depends on the person next to you, regardless of race, religion, politics or previous experiences.

The five-day processing experience consisted of a series of activities to destroy the individual and build a unit, a team. We all, ate marched, exercised, took physical examinations, got haircuts, were issued the same quantity and quality of uniforms, went to bed; and got up at the same time. A final phase of the processing centered around aptitude and vocational testing. This process helped match soldier's skills and abilities with the peculiar needs of the armed services. Once this phase was completed, these strangers with whom one was beginning to develop trust were transferred to another military facility to complete basic training.

I was transferred to Camp Gordon GA for basic training where I excelled and was chosen by the training cadre to attend leadership training school, after I had completed the eight weeks of basic training. The Leadership Training School, the precursor to the Army Special Forces, was rigorous, extremely competitive and a great test of one's physical, mental and emotional endurance. Of the twenty-one men selected for leadership training school, I was the only African American solider chosen from my training battalion. Of the eight men who graduated, I received the second highest score. Those who successfully completed Leadership Training were authorized to wear a distinguishing cuff around one's left sleeve.

The next phase of training was "military occupational specialty" (MOS). I was assigned to the army camp at San Louis Obispo, CA for a sixteen-week "Carrier Repeater" school. Soldiers with this MOS were trained to provide communications from command central to the fighting units on the battle field. It did not take the North Koreans military long to discover that if you cut the communication link between the unit commander and the fighting forces on the front lines, the unit was ineffective.

Soldiers with a "Carrier Repeater" military occupation specialty were living approximately seventy-one days after being deployed in battle.

By the grace of God, I was selected to be a military teacher. My responsibility now was to train others for this important role. This assignment allowed me to avoid participating on the battle field during the Korean War.

Although, President Harry S. Truman had issued Executive Order 9981, July 26, 1948, ending segregation in the armed services, minorities still endured harsher treatment, sometimes denied equal opportunities for advancement, and were given opportunities to compete for some positions. Soldiers who served in combat were promoted rapidly because of the high rate of American casualties. It was very difficult for non-combat service members to advance. In August of 1953 the Army Post newspaper announced, there was a competitive examination for promotion to the rank of corporal. I entered the competition and made the highest score. The next day my photo appeared on the front page of the Post newspaper. When I was interviewed for the story, and asked; "How is it, you have never participated in combat and yet scored higher than anyone else?" I replied, "My parents instilled in me, that I was no better than any one else, but I was just as good. In living up to their expectations, I was a little better than the others this time." Being the only African American in the 836 Signal Corp battalion at that time, my promotion surprised everyone except me. This promotion was another example of what happens when all people are given an equal chance to participate.

President Truman's Executive Order did not end the racist attitudes and comments that Black service men and women endured. The evening after my promotion and the Post news article; a group of servicemen from my company and I, journeyed to a bar in downtown Seattle, WA to celebrate my promotion. We were all in dress uniform. As soon as we were all seated, the bartender came over, pointed to me and said, "We don't serve him in here." To which the Sargent replied, "Then you can't serve any of us." This was a blatant reminder of what some of us had experienced all our lives, to defend and uphold the Constitution of the United States of America. What some citizens take for granted, others are subjected to insults, discrimination, humiliation and in some places, refusal of services.

When my active tour of duty was ending, in December 1953, my company commander, a captain ordered me to his office for a formal review of my career goals, and to recruit me for Officer's Candidate

School. In short, I was told with your aptitude, skills and ability to lead, you will make a great officer in the United States Army. He promised to write a letter to the Secretary of the Army ensuring my acceptance into OCS and my success would all but be assured. I listened carefully and politely, thanked the Captain for his assessment but declined to accept the offer for Officers Candidate School.

A month before my active duty ended, I was ordered back to company's headquarters and given another Officer Candidate School recruitment lecture. After I again declined the offer, to my surprise, the Captain stated, "You have too much going for you. Get out of this army, complete your education and make a life for yourself." Again, I thanked him, saluted and returned to my work station feeling that I had demonstrated that someone from "over the river" had succeeded because he was given a chance.

On Friday, February 12, 1954, I was discharged from active military service at Fort Lewis Washington, near Seattle. I was wiser, and had demonstrated that my parents were right; I was as good as anyone else. I could compete, and in some cases excel with anyone. The two years of active duty helped prepare me for service in the wider world.

CHAPTER 5

TRANSITIONING BACK INTO CIVILIAN LIFE

---◆---

I arrived home at midnight, Saturday, February 13 and joined the family for 11:00 o'clock worship service the following morning. This was a strange time. It seemed as if I was going back to an earlier, more primitive period. Everything seemed slower; old acquaintances seemed not to make sense. Former grade school mates had matured, got married and were raising families. Most of the young men my age were working on plantations or eking out a living on small family farms or other dead-end jobs in Monticello.

By the end of the first week at home with my parents; I informed them that I would reenroll in college and pursue a career as a teacher. My parents were thrilled. My oldest brother was in the army, stationed in Germany with an artillery company. My sister was in the hospital when I returned from service and my youngest brother was matriculating at FAMU. Living at home with my father and mother seemed inappropriate. However, my parents were eager to hear about my experiences in the armed services.

Within a few days after being released from active duty I purchased a 1950 Chevrolet. One of the first trips outside the county was to visit FAMU in Tallahassee to continue my education. I learned the earliest possible date I could enroll was the summer session which began the second week in June. I had nearly four months of "down time." I really became restless and was searching for direction. The friends with whom I grew up in rural Jefferson County before I was drafted into military service, all seemed to be headed in the wrong direction. They all, both males and females, seemed headed in a downward spiral. They had no goals, no purpose, no outlook for a better future. Their worldview was centered around existing in the community as it was. They never dreamed of a different community with better schools, better jobs, better social services, and a community where everyone would have an equal opportunity to rise above their present socio-economic status.

Every effort to engage my peers around these kinds of issues were met with indifference, at best, and sometimes with hostility. I felt like a stranger among the very people I had grown up with and knew all my life. The young woman whom I had dated prior to military service seemed to have retrogressed. Her conversations were intellectually poverty stricken, and we held little in common.

Fifteen days of idleness grew old very quick. I hired on with a bridge construction company headquartered in Perry, FL, a rigidly segregated town. The construction foreman had recently been discharged from the Marine Corps. As former military men, he and I made a good team. Although, every county in which we worked was segregated, I moved up in the company chain of command and became a team leader.

In Cross City, Dixie County Florida, I was the team leader for a racially diverse group of men. On my team was a middle-aged white man from the local community, Cross City. The crew was sent three miles away to haul a load of building sand. This guy refused to work stating, "No N----- is going to tell me what to do." He watched as the truck was loaded; and when everyone climbed aboard the truck to return to our work site, I ordered him off. When we arrived at the job site, I reported to the foreman, we were one man short because he refused to work; therefore, he was ordered off the truck. When this local man arrived, the foreman immediately and publicly fired him.

Some of the older black men on the job site became uneasy, frightened about this incident. They thought a local white group would try to get revenge. Many of the white men believed that black men should not be in leadership position, especially over white people. I worked hard, was always punctual, demonstrated concern for each member of the team and treated everyone fairly. I knew leaders must earn respect and it must be done day in and day out.

By March of 1954, approximately one month after returning home, I invited a young woman from "over the river," the east side of the Aucilla River to attend a movie with me one weekend. The next weekend we had dinner together, and by June we were engaged to be married. Rose and I were married July 18, 1954. The woman who became my wife was self-employed as a cosmetologist. She envisioned a better life, a different world; and she demonstrate a willingness to work to help make things better for ourselves and for others.

Mrs. Rose Proctor

By the time we got married, I was matriculating at Florida Agricultural and Mechanical University again. This environment was rich, stimulating and fulfilling. My wife worked as a hair stylist and the last two years of college passed swiftly. On June 3, 1956, I marched across the stage at FAMU and received a Bachelor of Science degree. I was the first in my family, and the first African American "over the river" in the eastern part of Jefferson County to attain this milestone. Two weeks later I entered graduate school pursuing a Master of Education degree.

On the afternoon of August 2, I was invited to Florida State Director of Vocational Agriculture's office for a job interview. On entering the office, I was congratulated for the excellent way I had conducted the State New Farmers of America's Convention (segregated unit to the Future Farms of America) approximately fifteen days earlier.

Then, I was asked, "Do you plan to teach vocational agriculture in Florida?"

My reply was a curt short one, "Yes."

This was followed by another question from the director, "Why haven't you filled out an application?"

I replied, "I was told by the dean of the school of agriculture at FAMU that there were absolutely no jobs available in Florida."

To impress upon me that he made the decisions regarding hiring vocational agriculture teachers in Florida, he said, "The dean doesn't know everything."

After that power play was over, I was then told, "A superintendent is waiting to interview you in my other office."

I walked into another office, was greeted warmly and the first statement made by Suwanee County's (Live Oak, Florida) Superintendent of Public Instruction was, "You look young to be graduating from college, are you confident that you can manage high school boys?"

I replied, "Sir, perhaps Mr. Woods, the State Director did not tell you how smooth the convention was planned and executed two weeks ago at the FAMU campus where I was responsible for nearly five hundred boys from throughout the state. Also, I served as a military teacher in the U. S. Army. I am confident, I can do an outstanding job with students in your county."

"You sound convincing," was his reply. Then as if, trying to test my professionalism, I was asked; "Vocational Agriculture teachers usually work longer hours than other teachers; if it is time to go home and a report is due in my office the next morning, what do you do?"

I replied, "Hourly workers stop when it is time to stop. Professionals stop when the task is completed."

The superintendent shook my hand and said, "Welcome aboard."

CHAPTER 6

THE JOYS AND CHALLENGES OF TEACHING

———◆———

On August 22, 1956, I joined the faculty of Douglass High School in Live Oak, FL as a teacher of vocational agriculture. My salary for that year was $3,600. Teaching agriculture in high schools were authorized by the Smith-Hughes National Vocational Education Act of 1917. It was an act of the United States Congress that promoted vocational education in agriculture, trades, industry and home economics.

One of the things that impressed me about vocational agriculture was the additional interest my vocational agriculture teachers demonstrated when I was in high school. In addition to mastering the concepts of learning, one had to demonstrate mastery by producing a crop, or making steps to enter the house, or raising chicken, or pigs. In other words, vocational agriculture teachers visited the home of each student and helped the student decide which project would enhance the quality of life for that family.

Let me give two examples: First, if a student decided to grow vegetables he/she had to select the proper soil, test it, estimate the cost of seeds, fertilizer, etc. all before the teacher would approve the project. These steps helped the students plan, use math skills, write clearly and select a project that was beneficial to his/her family.

Secondly, if a student wanted to grow baby chickens for food that student had to plan the entire project. Among the steps she must consider before spending money is the cost of housing the chicks, cost of the baby chicks, feed cost, estimated electrical and water costs and the approximate labor cost. These are some of the steps my students mastered in my vocational agriculture classes. Also, it was a joy to sit with a student as he explained his/her proposed project to their parents. This kept the parent engaged in their child's education and built a trusting relationship between parent, student and teacher.

In addition, vocational agriculture students were members of a national organization called 'New Farmers of American." In 1956 this was the African American segregated equivalent to the "Future Farmers of America." This organization fostered public speaking, critical thinking, livestock judging and other competitive educational activities to help make students well rounded citizens. The first year I taught a student from Douglass High School won first place in the public speaking contest.

Live Oak, Florida is the place where in 1955, a black woman killed a prominent white obstetrician in his office on a Sunday morning, allegedly because he had impregnated her and refused to perform an abortion.

That first school year passed swiftly with two major events that made a lasting mark in my life. November 1, 1956, a son was born to our family.

Also, in May 1957, my students were participating in the New Farmers of America State Convention where I had planned and executed the convention the previous year. The Vocational Agriculture Department of Douglass High School was rated as one of the outstanding programs in the state of Florida. The same state director who one year earlier had recommended me for the position in Live Oak, now recommended me for a similar position in Delray Beach-Palm Beach County, Florida. There was an immediate increase in salary of two thousand eighty dollars ($2080.00)   with increased entrepreneurial opportunities in the county for my wife.

Two years later we moved into our new home and my wife opened her very own hair styling solon. I made excellent progress professionally. Within three years I had become tenured in the Palm Beach County Public School system and took on many civic responsibilities in the community, such as voter registration, working with the Delray Beach Civic Association and the Boy Scouts of America.

My position as a vocational agriculture teacher provided opportunities for me to visit the home of every student in my classes. There were several students living in less than ideal situations. This was especially true for the students who were bussed in from the more rural communities of the county. They were ashamed for their teacher to visit them. I shared with my students that I grew up on a plantation and was a living example that where you live as a youth did not determine one's worth as a unique individual.

Two students in my classes who live on a plantation wanted to build fancy projects to decorate the yard, such as a concrete bench because other students were building concrete benches. After my first visit, I was able to help these two students decide to build an out-door toilet. After the design phase of the project, we all knew that the families were not financially able to purchase the building materials. I as teacher, was able to secure the building materials from building supply companies in the county.

Most students, after their project was completed, wanted to display them for others in the school to see. However, the students building the out-door toilets put their uncle's name on the project. Once the project was completed and erected at the home of these students who were ashamed of their teacher visit, these two boys and their vocational agriculture teacher became heroes to their families. These types of experiences represent the joys of teaching.

Most students who elected or were encouraged by their parents to participate in vocational agriculture courses performed better in the core subjects of the curriculum. This was true because students were able to see relationships between mathematics, biology, botany, chemistry and English. Students were able to see the interconnectedness of these subjects to life in the real world. It was a real joy to see the "ah ha" moment in a student when math made sense for the first time because he had to figure the cost of supplies or why it was important to write a clear sentence to explain how his project would enhance the quality of life for his/her family.

There were also some challenges. Some liberal art professionals acted as if vocational education was a dumping ground for the students who did not do well in other parts of the curriculum; therefore, those students were assigned to vocational agriculture courses. In those cases, students acted out because they resented being in vocational agriculture classes.

Teaching gave me opportunities to mold and shape lives. There are times, even now, when men and women greet me and tell of life changes they made because our paths crossed many years ago. This brings great joy and a sense of fulfillment only surpassed, for me, by the pastoral ministry.

OVER THE RIVER: MY JOURNEY HOME

CHAPTER 7

MY BURNING BUSH EXPERIENCE

———◆———

Teaching high school students was a time of upward mobility, professionally and economically, but it also was a time of searching for life's deeper meaning. Our young son added significance to life but there was still a deep yearning for purpose and meaning. Outwardly, I appeared to be thriving, but inwardly, I was unsure and convinced that God willed me to move in a different direction. Deep within, I yearned to find answers to life's deeper questions: Why am I here? What is my purpose in life? Am I really doing what God wants me to do?

I became increasingly active in Delray Beach's local Saint Paul African Methodist Episcopal Church. As a lay person, I served in practically every position in the church; assumed leadership position in the West Palm Beach District of the A. M. E. Church trying to satisfy that spiritual yearning that gnawed at my inner core. After many agonizing days and nights, I made an appointment with my pastor, the Reverend John D. Edwards, a giant of a man. Although Reverend Edwards was large in statue, he was warm, loving, gentle and kind.

After a few minutes of small talk, in his study, about my family and the Sunday school class I taught each week, I said to Pastor Edwards, "Pastor I think the Lord has called me to preach."

Reverend Edwards responded, "You think the Lord has called you to preach, go and pray for two weeks and let's talk about this again." At the close of his statement he stood, and I took that as a signal that the conference in his study was over. I left the pastors' study with mixed feelings. On the one hand, I was relieved, I had shared my spiritual struggle with my pastor. On the other hand, I was unsure that my pastor's action was a rejection of my spiritual struggles or a rejection of me, or worse, both.

Two or three days later around the dinner table one evening, I told my wife, "The Lord has called me to preach and I cannot go on acting otherwise. I am unable to sleep, and I have to share with you what's going on in my life."

My wife responded, "I have known this for a long time. We have to do what the Lord wants us to do."

There was a period of silence and then we embraced each other, and she said, "We are in this together."

Hearing those words was encouraging, and reassuring. At least, I knew my wife identified with my struggle and immediately she included herself in my struggles. This gave me the assurance, I had the support of the one person who I would need to make the biggest sacrifice in my vocational ministry.

The date pastor Edwards had set for a follow up conference with me arrived. This time, I was certain. I was confident of my calling; my vocation was to preach the gospel. So, this time I entered the pastor study with self-assurance. I said, "Pastor Edwards, I am confident, God has called me to preach the gospel."

I also said, "I have tried to ignore this deep inner pull, to devote my life to do the will of God. I know that I will never find inner peace unless I yield to do God's will for my life."

When I finished speaking Pastor Edwards stood and walked around his desk and said, "Let us pray." When he ended his prayer a calm, quiet, peace rested in my spirit and in my soul.

The pastor said, "I listened carefully to your words two weeks ago when you were here, and you said, "I think I have been called to preach." He continued, "This is a vocation one needs to be certain about. You do not need to think."

To my surprise, pastor Edwards said, "I had discerned this call on your life from the day I met you. The Sunday in July 1957, I saw this in you and prayed that your faith would increase to the point where you acknowledged God's plan for your life." He also said, "I am setting Wednesday night, May 16, 1961, 7:00 o'clock, as the date you will preach your initial sermon. Then we will convene a Church

Conference and the members of the congregation will vote to recommend you to the Quarterly Conference for a license to preach.

Wow, I thought, what if this doesn't pan out? Does this mean that I could fail even before I begin? The following Sunday, Pastor Edwards announced, during the morning worship service, "Brother James Proctor will preach his 'trial' sermon two weeks from now during the Wednesday night bible study."

The seventeen-days passed swiftly. And Wednesday night, May 16, 1961 found me in my usual place, at Saint. Paul African Methodist Episcopal Church, 119 NW Fifth Avenue, Delray Beach, Florida. This night, however, was different. Never had I felt the deep sense of urgency, a sense of responsibility a sense that I was yielding to the power of God.

Prior to leaving home to attend that special event; I opened the mail that had come that day. There were several congratulatory letters in the mail and a telegram from the principal of the Elementary School. These encouraging statements were greatly appreciated

Although I had spent many Wednesday nights at Saint Paul in bible study, this night was unique. This night was special. It was my public response to a higher power. It was my "burning bush" experience.

I arrived at the church at approximately 6:45 p. m. and went immediately to the pastor's study. At 6:59 Pastor Edwards led the way into the sanctuary. He directed me to sit on the front pew at the right of the chancellery. There were several people in my life who also knew this was a special time for me. In addition to my wife, among others were my mother who had traveled from Tampa, FL to be present that night. Faculty members with whom I worked at Carver High School were present. Also, to my surprise, there were students in Vocational Agriculture classes also in attendance that night.

The traditional order of service was followed and when it was time for the sermon, I was invited to the pulpit. When I finished, I was instructed to take the same seat again with the lay people. This seemed strange, at that time. However, I came to understand later that one is a lay person in the African Methodist Episcopal Church until one is ordained.

My sermon was based on the biblical account in Matthew 8:28-29 where Jesus asked his disciples, "Who do people say that I am?" They responded by reporting what others were saying. They reported that some people are saying that you are John the Baptist. Others are saying, you are Elijah and still others are saying, you are one of the prophets. Then Jesus confronted his followers directly, asking specifically, "What about you, who do you say that I am?" The scripture says, Peter declared, "You are the Christ, the Son of the living God."

I tried to impress on the congregation that night, we all need to know and confess for ourselves, as Peter did, that Jesus is the Messiah, the Son of God. The Christian faith is not based on what others say about Jesus the Son of God. The Christian faith is not in itself a group activity. The Christian faith in its most fundamental sense is individualistic, it is personal, it is what each one of us believes and is willing to act on. The Christian faith is not what others say about Jesus. Each one of us must develop a personal, dynamic relationship with Jesus Christ. Real faith can never be based solely on the opinions of others. Genuine, authentic, faith must be built on personal confessions and a growing relationship with God as revealed in Jesus Christ. William H. Bathurst captured the faith that Peter expressed in a Christian Hymn, number 428 in the African Methodist Episcopal Church Hymnal:

Of for a faith that will not shrink, though pressed by every foe,
That will not tremble on the brink, of any earthly woe.

That will not murmur nor complain beneath the chastening rod,
But, in the hour of grief of pain will lean upon its God.

A faith that shines more bright and clear when tempest rage without;
That when in danger knows no fear, in darkness feels no doubt;

Lord, give me such a faith as this' and then, what ever may come,

I'll taste, even now, the hallowed bliss of an eternal home.

After that night, things seemed different. I became more sensitive to my environment. As I traveled Palm Beach County roads and streets I saw things that I had not seen during the previous four years. I noticed the social interaction between diverse groups. An example of this was to drive on a major thoroughfare, the Dixie High Way, and see signs on "honky tonk" taverns, some painted in large black and white letters and some in red and white letters that said, "no niggers and Mexicans aloud." This disturbed me to my core. I scheduled a conference with my pastor and shared my outrage. Pastor Edwards said, "There are somethings that only time will change, and I recommend that you not get involved." This was not the answer I had expected from my pastor. But I felt obligated to follow his instructions at that time.

By January of 1962, I shared the news with my wife that I had been accepted in Turner Theological Seminary in The Interdenominational Theological Center, Atlanta, GA as a student to pursue a professional degree in pastoral ministry. Rose, my wife, seemed shocked! She reminded me of how we had sacrificed to buy our new house and her cosmetology business was now prospering, plus our son would be entering first grade. We talked late into the night without convincing each other that the course I was embarking on was for our mutual good.

In one final effort to dissuade me, Rose asked, "How are we going to meet the mortgage payments and meet all the other expense associated with graduate education?"

I replied, "We will do it the same way we have done it before, when I was running from what God wanted me to do."

She paused for a moment, came over and put her arms around my shoulders and said, "I am going with you." We'll close the shop, lease the house and we will all move to Atlanta together."

A month later, I called my father who was pastoring an A. M. E. Church in Tampa to tell him about my decision to pursue graduate theological education. Expecting to hear a word of encouragement, instead dad said, "Boy, you have enough education. You just need to preach." I thanked him and informed him that I was resigning my position as a tenured faculty member in the Palm Beach County Public School system effective June 30th.

The days, weeks and months passed quickly. And instead of waiting until September to go to Atlanta, I enrolled in Atlanta University for an eight-week summer session. The three hours of ancient history and a course in ancient literature helped me to refocus from a scientific, biological perspective to a philosophical, faith perspective. In addition, the eight weeks session in Atlanta University during the summer of 1962, gave me an opportunity to adjust from being a teacher to be a student, on the other side of the desk. That summer in Atlanta University also gave me an opportunity to find employment to support my family, find housing and become familiar with the city. My burning bush experience, my call to ministry, unlike Moses in the Hebrew Scriptures, was not instantaneous. It was a gradual unfolding, it was an inner, unrelenting urge, a revelation that God has chosen me to be a preacher, teacher, and leader for Him.

OVER THE RIVER: MY JOURNEY HOME

CHAPTER 8

YEARS OF PREPARATION

———◆———

September 1962 arrived, and we packed our clothing, rented a U-Hall trailer and headed to Atlanta five or six days before classes began. I reported, as instructed, to the seminary business manager to pick up keys to a one-bedroom apartment for which I had applied, only to be given the keys to an efficiency apartment. The difference was major. The efficiency apartment consisted of a kitchenette, a bathroom, a small desk, one chair and a foldaway bed. The efficiency apartment was very inadequate for three of us; two adults and a six-year old son. The one bedroom apartment contained a kitchen with stove and refrigerator, table and chairs, one furnished bedroom and the fold away bed which was adequate for our family. We were living comfortably in a three-bedroom house in Delray Beach, FL.

Tired and exhausted from driving and disappointed, we slept there one night and moved across town to an older housing complex owned by Gammon Theological Seminary. Were we to have lived in the Gammon housing complex meant, I would have a thirty-minute drive each day to classes, and I would not have immediate access to the library nor the educational and cultural benefits of living and mingling with members of the campus community. This housing arrangement would not work. This was a low moment. I immediately thought about my experience when I enrolled as a freshman in undergraduate school when the scholarship I was supposed to receive was awarded to another student.

Two days later, my wife, while walking, met the seminary president's wife and shared our disappointment regarding the housing arrangements. The next day, the same business manager who refused to honor my housing contract called to inform me that a one-bedroom apartment was now available. We moved into a one-bedroom apartment on the Interdenominational Theological Center's (ITC) campus. The apartment was not spacious, but it was adequate for our purposes. It was located at 641 Beckwith Street, South, Atlanta, GA, adjacent to Morris Brown College, near Clark University, Morehouse College and Atlanta University. Also, our son's elementary school was adjacent to the ITC's campus. This was an ideal location.

The seminary experience was extremely challenging. It stretched me intellectually and forced me to rethink many of long-held views about the Christian faith. Being exposed to exegetical and hermeneutical intervention methodologies equipped me to minister to a religious and socially diverse world.

Some of the deals about faith, at times, shook me to my core. My original interpretation of scriptures was often challenged. What I had accepted as facts were often called in to question.

The first semester in seminary was a major adjustment. My previous intellectual discipline was in the biological sciences. Reality was determined by what one could observe, touch, dissect, and test under a variety of conditions. Theology was different. My Sunday school view of God was inadequate in more ways than one. First, it was inadequate when bad things happened. The experience about the housing is an example; I had made the deposit on a one-bedroom apartment since June, was assured that I would be assigned to a one-bedroom apartment and arrived on campus in September and no apartment. Also, my Sunday school view of God did not work well toward maintaining a strong, healthy marriage the first year in seminary. I attended classes all day, worked in the afternoon and early evening, studied late into the night, sometimes all night. Although, my wife and I loved each other, I failed to recognize and compensate for the stressors that are associated with: leaving familiar support systems, moving into a new community, our son entering school for the first time. Also, the economic situation was bleak.

Prior to seminary, we both had good incomes. Now we had to live by a strict budget, barely earning enough to purchase groceries, seldom able to see a movie or go out to dinner. Things were financially difficult and that made life miserable for my wife and me. Some would say if the Lord calls you to preach he will make everything alright. God does not, in my opinion, do for us what we can do for ourselves.

I was immersed in study and my new position; my wife was left to make the adjustments alone. We were living in a new community, without the comforts of our home, friends and support systems back in Florida. The friends and support systems for my wife were not there. She was no longer the entrepreneur, calling her own shots as a hair stylist, banking her own money, making decisions about her business and deciding which new restaurant we would try this weekend. She was alone. With the help of a sensitive professor who sensed that something was wrong, we were able to work through these problems and enabled to move forward together as a cohesive family unit. This was a dark, low point in our marriage.

At the beginning of my second year in seminary, things were going well.

Rose, my wife, Reginald, our son, and I were actively engaged in the ministry of Flipper Temple AME Church, on Fair Street, Atlanta. The pastor, The Reverend and Mrs. Julius C. Williams were genuinely warm, mentoring, encouraging and supportive. That congregation embraced and nurtured us throughout the remaining years of study.

Midway through that second year, on a recommendation from the Reverend Doctor Josephus Cone, President of AME students at ITC; I was employed as the Associate Director of Religious Activities at Morris Brown College. My responsibilities included planning and conducting religious activities for students, faculty and staff. I was thrilled to be recommended and appointed to this position. It meant I no longer had to leave ITC's campus drive downtown Atlanta, park, which was expensive, work until 9:00 p.m., drive back to campus and prepare for class the next morning.

My new position allowed me to walk from the ITC campus to my office on the Morris Brown College campus. The new position also gave me immediate access to men and women of renown stature in the Atlanta University education community. In addition, the position as College Minister gave me opportunities to put into to practice immediately some of the new theories I was learning in seminary classes. The interaction with college students, faculty and members of the administrative staff was enriching. In addition, the educationally stimulating environment was very different than the hustle and bustle of managing a crew in the Receiving Department of Davidson Department Store on Peachtree Street in downtown Atlanta.

Another benefit of serving as college minister was the freedom to interact with men and women in similar position throughout the Atlanta University community. The Atlanta University community consisted of the following institutions of higher learning: Atlanta University, Clark College (University now), Morehouse College, Morris Brown College, Spelman College and the Interdenominational Theological Center. The Atlanta University community, at that time, was perhaps the largest consecration of African American scholars in the United States. One could expect to hear some new philosophical or theological debate in nearly every restaurant, barber shop or beauty parlor in the city. In short, the period between September 1962 and May 1965 was a time of great intellectual growth for me despite some family adjustments. That is, I forgot, that first year, to provide nurture and support to my wife.

Looking back, the seminary journey was a bitter-sweet experience. I learned a whole new way of experiencing reality. Seminary was that period when I had more questions than answers. It was a time of searching and exploring. It was a time when "over the river" meant something more than a physical location. "Over the River" became a launching pad for a new reality.

Ontologically, I seriously began to ponder the meaning of God, the creative source of the cosmos. This was the time, when I pondered, like others before me: "Who am I?" "What is my purpose in life?" "What can I really do to make the world a better place?" "What is my responsibility to those closest to me?" These are some of the questions

I wrestled with unceasingly, at times, during my seminary days. These are questions with which I still wrestle.

In addition to the intellectual growth, I learned a lot about myself and the responsibility of marriage. I learned to always be mindful that I was not alone. But God had put my wife and me together as a family unit; therefore, my ministry would rise, or fall based on my concern, love and care for my wife. This concern, love and care was not based on what I said to my wife but what I demonstrated day in and day out.

A caring homiletics professor helped me to see that my ministry would always be more authentic, more rooted in Christian love if I demonstrated the importance of family. I learned under the tutelage of this one sensitive professor that if I demonstrated my love and care for my family the people whom I was fortunate enough to serve would sense this and many would imitate my actions. I left seminary with a healthier marriage, a marriage that has lasted for more than six decades.

To my surprise, two months before I graduated, I was invited to deliver the baccalaureate sermon at Carver High School, the place I had resigned three years earlier to attend seminary. This was quite an honor. However, the baccalaureate sermon gave me the opportunity to reflect, also on the next chapter in my life. In a real sense, I was commencing on a new journey, launching a vocation, new career, responding to new vocational demands. Seminary ended May 1965, my family and I returned home to Delray Beach, Florida, strengthened by the experience.

CHAPTER 9

MY ORDINATION

My conversion mentioned earlier in this book was a spiritual high mountain in my life. The acknowledgement of the call to ministry was a struggle of faith, and the gumption to publicly declare that call to those who know you best; one's immediate and extended family members, professional colleagues and associates required a great deal of faith. In the African American community, in many instances ministers are viewed differently. After I publicly declared my call to preach, often I was called to settle scriptural disputes.

From the time I preached the initial sermon, life with my friends was different. My in-laws also treated me differently. At every gathering in their home, I was asked to bless the food, give the prayer and or read the scripture. I was now more than their son-in-law, I was a minister held in high esteem. The first ten to twelve months this made me feel very uncomfortable. However, I came to accept this cultural view of how others saw me and tried to always be prepared to represent the high calling to which I had been chosen.

In the African Methodist Episcopal Church, the call to the ministry does not automatically qualify one as a minister. Usually there is a four to five-year process from admission to an Annual Conference to ordination as an Itinerant Elder. My journey took four years but there were some challenges along the way.

I will mention one of the challenges I had to overcome in the quest to be ordained an Itinerant Elder. My initial sermon was May 16, 1961. I was licensed by the Presiding Elder in June of that same year and admitted to the South Florida Annual Conference in October 1961.

September 1962, I enrolled in Seminary and was struggling to make ends meet financially, plus adjusting to seminary life. The bishop presiding over the eleventh episcopal district-Florida- also had an office in Atlanta, GA, approximately four blocks from the Interdenominational Theological Center's campus, where I was matriculating.

Two weeks after entering seminary, in addition to the housing boom doggie, I realized I would not have money to travel back to South Florida to attend the Annual Conference which is a requirement. I therefore made a 1:00 P. M. appointment to meet the bishop of Florida to explain my situation, and request permission to meet the Atlanta North Georgia Annual Conference instead. Bishop Sherman Lawrence Greene kept me waiting for one hour and fifteen minutes before inviting me into his office. I introduced myself and explained my dilemma. Bishop Greene's reply was immediate and unsympathetic; "If you can't attend the Annual Conference to answer the roll call, you will not advance. You will just have to wait for another year." Dejected, I left the bishop's office disappointed with his insensitivity, his action, and the fact that he had shown little regard to my situation.

I was led by the Holy Spirit to transfer my membership from Saint Paul African Methodist Episcopal Church, Delray Beach, FL to Flipper Temple African Methodist Episcopal Church, Atlanta, GA. I met the next session of the Atlanta North Georgia Annual Conference, presided over by Bishop Ernest Lawrence Hickman and was ordained an Itinerant deacon because of my standing in seminary. That decision made it possible for me to be considered for a ministerial position at Morris Brown College about which I will share later in this book. In 1964, I was ordained an Itinerant Elder in the African Methodist Episcopal Church. This truly was a high point in my life.

The ordination liturgy made an unforgettable impact on me. At times during my ministry when I have felt extremely tired or wanted to take a short cut, the words of that ordination service have strengthened my resolve to put forth every effort to live up to the vows I had at the altar of an African Methodist episcopal church more than a half century ago. Some of the words of the elder's ordination still motivate me to do all that I can to live out my commitment to God and to God's people whom I have been privileged to serve.

Among the processes one must satisfactory complete prior to ordination are: a battery of psychological and physical tests, criminal background investigation, an annual test of educational advancement in an accredited seminary, and also an in-depth interview by a group of elders called the Board of Examiners. Come the day of ordination, the bishop asks the members of the Annual Conference, "If any of you know any impediment or crime . . . for which he/she ought not to be received into this holy ministry, let them come forth in the name of God and show what the crime or impediment is." That solemn moment is followed by "The Collect", The Epistle and The Gospel lessons. The next phase of the ordination is what I call the obligation or the oath of office:

You have heard, as well in your private examination and in the exhortation, which was just made to you, and in the writings of the apostles, of what dignity and how great importance this office is, to which you are now called. And now again we exhort you in the name of our Lord Jesus Christ that you have in remembrance into how high a dignity and to how weighty an office you are called; that is to say to be messengers, watchers, and stewards of the Lord; to teach and to admonish, to feed and provide to the Lord's family; to seek for Christ's sheep that are dispersed abroad, and for his children who are in the midst of this evil world that they may be saved through Christ forever.

Have always, therefore, printed in your remembrance how great treasure is committed to your charge. For they are the sheep of Christ which he bought with his death, and for whom he shed his blood. The church and congregation, whom you must serve, are his spouse and his Body. And if it should happen the same church or any member thereof, do take any hurt or hindrance by reason of your negligence, you know the greatness of the fault, and also the horrible punishment that will ensue. Wherefore consider within yourselves the end of the ministry towards the children of God, toward the Spouse and the Body of Christ, and see that you never cease your labor, your care, and diligence until you have done all that lies in you, according to your duty, to bring all such as are or shall be committed to your charge unto that agreement in the faith, and to that ripeness and perfectness of age in Christ, that there may be no place left among you, either for error in religion or for viciousness in life.

Forasmuch then is your office is both of so great excellence, and of so great difficulty, you see with how great awe and study you ought to apply yourselves, and neither you yourselves offend, nor be occasion that others offend. Howbeit you cannot have a mind and will thereunto of yourselves for that will, and ability are given of God alone; therefore, you ought, and have need, to pray earnestly for God's Holy Spirit. And seeing that you cannot by other means compass the doing of so weighty a work pertaining to the salvation of people, with doctrine and exhortation taken out of the Holy Scriptures, and with a life agreeable to the same, consider how studious you ought to be in reading and learning the Scriptures and in framing the manners both of yourselves and of them that specially pertain to you, according to the rules of the same Scriptures; and for this self-same cause how you ought to forsake and set aside as much as you may all worldly care and studies.

We have good hope that you have all weighed and pondered with yourselves long before this time; and that you have clearly determined by God's grace to give yourselves to this office whereby it has pleased God to call you, so that as much as lies within you, you will apply yourselves wholly to this one thing and draw all your cares and studies this way, and that you will continually pray to God the Father by the mediation of our only Savior Jesus Christ, of the heavenly assistance of the Holy Spirit; that by daily reading and weighing of the Scripture you may wax riper and stronger in your ministry, and that you may so endeavor yourselves, from time to time, to sanctify the lives of you and yours, and to fashion them after the rule and doctrine of Christ that you may be wholesome and godly examples and patterns for the people to follow (The Doctrine and Discipline of the African Methodist Episcopal Church, 2016, P.653).

That sacred obligation and commitment have been my spiritual anchoring source; a frequent reminder of my commitment "to wax riper and stronger in ministry." There were parts of the liturgy I have never forgotten. The admonition by Bishop Ernest Lawrence Hickman to "Have always, therefore, printed in your remembrance how great treasure is committed to your charge. For they are the sheep of Christ which he bought with his death, and for whom he shed his blood." The liturgy, sermon, music and rays of sunlight piercing through stain glass windows at Saint Mark AME Church with the hand of the bishop and six other elders placed on my head left an unforgettable stamp in my spirit.

Since my ordination, I have tried to live up to the high demands of that office. I have grown and come to understand the demands of the gospel are greater than I can achieve. However, I am called to do my best, to never shirk from the responsibility of being the voice for the voiceless and to always work to help make this world the kingdom of our Lord.

I recall those ugly signs I encountered on cheap taverns along the Dixie Highway in Palm Beach County in 1961, immediately after acknowledging the call to ministry, "No N-----s and Mexicans allowed." At that time, I acquiesced to my pastor's advice, "There are some things time will change."

As I grew in faith, knowledge, gained skills in the last years of my ministry, I engaged those demons. My position with the New York State Council of Churches, ministering to migrants and seasonal farm workers, to the homeless in Jacksonville, FL, to youth arrested for minor, non-violent misdemeanors, improving the transportation system for the poorest in our city are some examples of my ministerial focuses. Yes, I have saved souls, baptized infants, youth and adults, provided pastoral care to thousands of individuals during my ministry. I have been responsible for thousands of dollars of apportionment (assessments), remodeled churches, purchased parsonages and built one of the finest facilities in the connection. However, some of the greatest thrills I have seen as a minister is a family moving into their own home, constructed with sweat equity, or the teen aged girl who was given a "civil citation" instead of an arrest record for picking up a seventy-nine cents candy bar. This young woman is now a Sargent in the U. S. Army. These kinds of accomplishments, by the grace of God, are tangible evidence of my accomplishments.

CHAPTER 10

THE SUMMER AFTER SEMINARY

---◆---

The summer of 1965, I was back home with a Master of Divinity degree, a wife, a son and a mortgage to pay, without a position to earn an income. And what was worse, my Annual Conference, the time when AME ministers receive pastoral appointments, did not convene until late October. Knowing the date of my Annual Conference, before graduating from seminary; I applied for a position with the New York State Council of Churches for the summer months. On May 12, 1965, I received a letter informing me that I had been accepted for a position as "Chaplain to seasonal agricultural workers" in Orleans County New York from June 1 to August 31, 1965. This position was intended for a minister to minister to farm workers while they harvested the crops of farmers. The workers were predominately African Americans from Dade, Indian River, Lee, Palm Beach (the same county where I lived), Polk, and St. Lucie Counties in Florida and Latinos from Mexico.

That three-month experience was an eye opener. The position was made possible by charitable donations from the white protestant church in Orleans County, payable to the New York State Council of

Churches. Some of the ministers whose churches supported this ministry, invited me to speak to their congregants during the regular 11:00 o'clock worship service.

In most churches in Orleans County the dominant group was farmers. I often centered my message around agricultural related ideas. Cornell University educated, vegetable, cherry and apple growers understood entomology, agronomy, horticultural and botanical terms. Many times, they disagreed with my theological position but could not dismiss me because I had intellectual credibility with them.

Some churches where I was invited to preach would shake the pastor's hand as they were leaving, as was the custom, but would refuse to shake my hand. These presentations gave me opportunities to invite senior high school and college students to join us in providing meaningful experiences for the farm workers children. Some of these students whose parents owned the farms had never met the children of the farm workers and had little knowledge of the deplorable living conditions their parents provided for the migrant families. Although, New York State had a strict housing code for seasonal farm workers, many farmers circumvented the law by housing one less person than the code required.

My three-month work as Chaplain for the New York Council of Churches ended on August 31, 1965. We had traveled hundreds of miles, visited every migrant camp, sixty-six of them in Orleans County; preached in five Protestant churches and met individually and in a group with most of the Catholic priests to explain our ministry. We had recruited twenty-seven volunteers who transported people to health care facilities, provided recreational and educational activities, and field trips for the children of farm workers. I completely fulfilled my responsibility to the people I was employed to serve.

I also fulfilled my responsibility to the Orleans County Migrant Ministry and the New York State Council of Churches by writing a comprehensive report. The report included a lot of statistics. Such as: number of miles traveled, number of camps visited, number of worship services conducted, individual counseling sessions, the number of local volunteers employed (volunteering) in the ministry etc. The form contained a blank space for recommendations. I documented all the work we had accomplished in three months. However, I concluded the report by expressing gratitude for the opportunity to serve the men and women, the unseen forces who contribute to our food supply. I also included a paragraph that suggested a summer chaplain was not the most effective way to minister to the large group of persons who annually came to harvest their crops.

Two weeks after returning to my home in Delray Beach, I received a phone call from a Presbyterian Pastor who was chair of the Migrant Ministry Committee. He thanked me for the report and stated, "Your report has caused some dynamic discussions regarding my first recommendation."

I asked, "Did the committee members read the complete statement?"

He replied, "Yes, but they think you were ungrateful that you were employed here with us."

I paused for a moment or two and then said, "Maybe it's good that I am back in Florida before they received the report." We both laughed and continued to discuss the contents of the report.

After the statistical section of the report, the first question asked, "What recommendations you have to improve the work to seasonal workers?"

My response to that inquiry, "The Migrant Ministry Committee should not employ another person during the summer to minister to seasonal agricultural workers and their families."

My statement went on to explain, with more than 60 different camps in Orleans County, it was impossible for any one person to do an adequate job of building meaningful, trusting, pastoral relationship with that many people in such a short time. Moreover, the statement clearly stated that if such a ministry were to have long-term benefits the "chaplain" needed to minister to both the migrants and the growers.

For too long, the pastors of white Protestant churches, largely supported by growers, decided what activities should be performed for farm workers who harvest the crops. The white pastors decided what should be done based on what they thought would keep the growers in their congregations happy. They never met with, planned nor sought to ascertain what the workers needed or wanted. The growers wanted a "chaplain" to keep the workers contented, but to do nothing that would upset the social equilibrium in the county.

It never occurred to the growers and pastors, or maybe it did, to ask the workers what services they needed most. In short, the Migrant Ministry Committee, with the full support of the New York State Council of Church planned for the ministry without ever consulting the workers as to the type of services they needed or wanted.

The farm workers, both African Americans and Latinos appreciated the worship services; but worship service after a long day's work was not the top three of four items on their list of needs. The farm workers identified a totally different litany of need: higher wages, better housing, access to health care services, wholesome educational activities for their children and a desire to get out of the transitory, migrant farm worker labor system. These were services that required a whole reorientation by the members of the committee and a full-time, long-term, dedicated, hard worker with a theological view toward empowering workers rather than pacifying them. In addition, to plan and implement this type of ministry would take longer than three months in the summer. It required a change in direction and a re-education of the sponsoring committee.

My recommendations also included the Migrant Ministry Committees of Orleans and Genesee Counties cease operating as Migrant Ministry Committees under the auspice of the New York State Council of Church and form a 501 C (3), tax-exempt, not-for-profit organization by the name of the Genesee-Orleans Ministry of Concern, Inc. The board of directors should be comprised of clergy, at least one former seasonal farm worker, farmers, and an attorney. I thought I had been faithful to the men and women who hired me but wanted to make it clear, what they were doing was hiring an unemployed seminarian to sooth their collective conscious and maintain the status quo. They were not doing much more.

To paraphrase one of Einstein phrases, to do the same thing and expect a different result is insane. Therefore, the migrant ministry as it was conducted in those two counties should end and a new model of ministry be implemented.

CHAPTER 11

MY FIRST PASTORATE

In mid-October 1965, Bishop Eugene Clifford Hatcher appointed me to the pastoral charge of Good Hope African Methodist Episcopal Church in Pensacola, FL. I knew my first pastoral appointment would not be economically enough to support my family. Therefore, I requested to be assigned to a church in the South Florida Conference where our home was located and where I had developed professional ties and social networks links with several individuals and groups. Pensacola was as far away from our home as I could be and still serve a church in Florida. The distance was approximately 650 miles. My request was denied, and I was told by Bishop Hatcher that this was the only appointment he was offering me. I protested and reminded him that according to the Doctrine and Discipline of the AME Church an itinerant elder could not be transferred out of one's conference without a ninety-day notice. His response was, "If you serve the Good Hope church for one year, I will transfer you back to the South Florida Conference." With that assurance, I reluctantly accepted the appointment.

When I informed my wife of the appointment we both cried tears of disappointment. I was the first seminary educated pastor that had been assigned to that congregation at that time, and I was the youngest pastor appointed to that church.

I drove from Delray Beach on a Wednesday, arriving at the church at approximately 7:30 in the evening to find about twenty people in choir rehearsal. I knelt at the altar rail, offered a prayer to God, rose, introduced myself, presented my certificate of pastoral appointment, and made brief remarks. I received the keys to the parsonage and went to bed.

A cursory inspection of the facilities the next morning revealed water stain in the church's ceiling, indicating a leaking roof, the restrooms were outdoors, the choir loft was too small and there was no office for the pastor. I knew immediately my first pastoral appointment would not be a cake walk. That appointment would test every tool in my kit.

As I drove back to Delray Beach on Thursday to get clothing, books and other essentials, I was in prayer that God would guide me as I undertook the pastoral responsibility of leading a congregation for the first time. I also was eager to share my findings with my wife who had sacrificed enormously for three years while I earned a professional degree. I had to be honest with myself; this was not the kind of appointment I thought I would receive. As I drove back toward

Delray Beach, I was filled with nervous excitement. My mind drifted between two poles; being honest with my wife about my disappointment and at the same time displaying a sense of optimism and expressing confidence that with God's help we could make a significant difference in the lives of the people I had been assigned to serve.

By the time I reached home, I was convinced that this was the assignment God wanted me to have. I realized, on faith journeys life is never easy and if the task was not difficult any other pastor could have been assigned to that pastoral charge. I was convinced that God had placed me there for a specific purpose. Yes, my outlook had changed when I reached my wife in Delray Beach.

I spent Friday preparing my first sermon for the people at Good Hope AME Church. This was different from preaching in the chapel services at Morris Brown College or in upstate New York to migrants or even in white protestant churches. These were people over whom I am now their shepherd. Their previous pastor had been with them for more than a decade. He was a dynamic, emotional preacher whose theology focused on a better life after a while. He was a local man who had grown up in the community. He was one of them. Pastor McNealy had now been promoted to a larger congregation, across town. He had several friends in the Good Hope congregation, some as far back as high school days. He was not formally educated and did not have the knowledge, skills and ability to plan and provide a comprehensive ministry for the entire congregation. Basically, my predecessor was an effective preacher who satisfied the parishioners preaching style. I could never match his oratorical skills. My strengths were teaching, pastoral care, leadership and counseling.

Therefore, my preparation for my first sermon focused on a familiar passage of Scripture: *"You are the salt of the earth; but if salt has lost its taste, how can its saltiness be restored? It is no longer good for anything but is thrown out and trampled underfoot. 14You are the light of the world. A city built on a hill cannot be hid"* *(Matthew 5:13-14 NRSV)*. My initial sermon was intended to help the people to see themselves as a saving, preserving, flavoring, illuminating force in a decaying, dark, gloomy world.

As Christians, and as a disciple of Christ each one of us are called to give hope, encouragement, and radiant love to all whom we encounter. We are called of God to work to build a better society. A failure to use our God given resources to help build a better community risked losing our capacity to influence others for good. I proclaimed, if we did not use our God-given gifts we would lose the saltiness of life and become no better than a footpath for travelers. I elaborated on verse 13 about "salt of the earth," and then focused on "light" in the text. The sermon was also intended to help each congregant see themselves, and the role each of us played in building a strong, vibrant, Christian community.

Our light was not a Sunday morning worship experience only; but it must shine in our homes, on our jobs, and on the play grounds. At the close of service, approximately half of the people in the congregation stood in line to welcome me. We, then were invited to dinner at one of the member's home.

Monday night was time for my first Official Board meeting. It was there I learned the minister's salary was fifty-five dollars ($55.00) per week. I said, publicly, I am disappointed that this congregation only pays it's minister so little. I promised to work harder than any previous pastor and demonstrate my desire to build a stronger congregation in that community. The first month of my ministry at Good Hope was spent in intense listen sessions. I visited nearly every home to hear about their pains, hopes and aspirations. These intense listening sessions gave me information that helped to plan a ministry that met the needs of the people.

Among the acute needs that surfaced during my listening campaign were the following: 1) replace the roof immediately, 2) install modern, indoor restrooms, 3) enlarge the choir loft, and 4) provide pastoral care for all members. In addition, I discovered, based on financial records for the last three years, only a very small percentage of members had supported the church financially.

Listening is almost a lost art. However, I believe people feel valued, appreciated and important when one listens to them. Each one of us has a story. And sometimes, we feel taken for granted when we never get the opportunity to be heard, to be listened to, to really be heard.

This listening process convinced me that some members were ashamed to be using outdoor facilities in 1965. Others thought the church could pay their pastor a better salary; and still others thought two or three families controlled every decision and were the gate keepers, impeding the progress of the congregation.

Six weeks after I arrived, I called a Church Conference to place before the congregation a plan of ministry for the year, and to organize the congregation. We elected most of the officers without opposition.

But one person, who had been identified as one of the controlling members stated, "If you elect (I'll call him Charlie Brown), I won't serve on the Board of Trustees."

I stated, "Based on the tallied votes cast and counted by the election committee, both you and Mr. Brown have been elected to serve as Trustees. Are you offering your resignation?"

He replied, "Yes."

As chair of the Church Conference, I asked for a motion to accept "Mr. Controller's" resignation. A motion was made, someone seconded it and the election was completed. During this initial church conference, the organization was finalized, and a budget was approved that included money to service a debt for the improvements identified above. I then implemented a serious study on stewardship, transparency, management, and accountability. The benefits were seen immediately. Our tithing and offerings tripled. The members felt good about themselves and Good Hope AME church became the "talk" in barber shops and beauty salons.

Meanwhile, shortly after I arrived in Pensacola, I was invited to preach at a union worship service with eleven other churches. A well-connected lay woman, who knew about the salary structure at Good Hope, heard me preach, asked in a private conversation, if I would consider working as a substitute teacher in Escambia County Public School System. I accepted the offer and worked almost the entire year at one Junior High School because of the illness of one teacher. God made it possible for us to survive economically during that year in my first pastoral charge.

The Lord blessed our ministry! New members were added to our church, all the physical improvements had been completed and our members were feeling good about themselves and their church. By February, we had paid all the apportionments for the entire year. However, I did not believe I should have to work two jobs to provide for my family. I called the bishop to inform him of our progress and to remind him of his promise, "if I would serve that congregation for one year, he would then appoint me to a pastorate in South Florida, near my home." Immediately, he said, "You will have to stay out there another year." Again, I reminded him of his promise when I accepted the appointment, if I would serve that congregation for one year, I would be appointed to a church in the South Conference. He again said I would have to serve the Good Hope congregation another year. I then said, "Bishop, I regret I must request a transfer from your jurisdiction, I am uncomfortable serving under a bishop who does not keep his promises." My statement was not welcomed. However, I believed I needed to be true to my God, my family and myself. To not insist on being respected, in my opinion, was to be a part of the problem. This I could not do. I believe if I do what is right, God will make a way for me. I had struggled financially now for four years. My wife had made significant sacrifices, I was not willing to ask more of her.

August 1, 1966, almost a year after making the recommendations to strengthen the ministry for seasonal workers and growers, I was contacted by the same individual who informed me of the committee's negative reaction to my report. He was curt and direct, asking if I would return to implement the recommendations I had made.

After being assured of at least a three-year commitment, I accepted the offer with some other negotiated modifications. Two major changes we negotiated: First, the Genesee-Orleans Ministry of

Concern, Inc. officially affiliate with the New York State Council of Churches to give it immediate credibility, and the benefits of its payroll and human resource systems. Secondly, the position of "Chaplain" be changed to "Associate Executive Director of the New York State Council of Churches."

The director of the New York State Council of Churches, headquartered in Syracuse, NY had received every report that I had made to the local Migrant Ministry Committee and was in support of my recommendations. My job description included community development, social justice and priestly activities for seasonal farm workers, their families and farmers in Genesee and Orleans counties, New York; and assist the director of the council with planning, organizing, and staffing migrant ministry activities in Western New York.

The months of August and September 1966 were filled with mixed emotions. I had found satisfaction in pastoral ministry and believed in my heart that I was making a positive impact on people's lives. I could sense positive changes in people's behavior. I also was having an impact in the larger community, especially among Escambia County public school teachers and younger clergy in the county. Among the services I provided to public school teachers was tutorial help in passing the Florida State Teacher's Examination. Each person with whom I worked successfully passed the examination.

The clergy were amazed at how quickly we were able to complete the renovations of the church facilities. Despite these accomplishments; three overriding factors necessitated me accepting the position in New York. First, my wife had made significant sacrifice for my career. I was not willing to prolong this economic state. During the four years she had abandoned her occupation. A second factor was the committee had instituted every recommendation I had made. I believed, I was the best person to implement my recommendations. A third factor, I had lost faith in my ecclesial leader. Therefore, I needed to accept a new position that removed me from his judicatory oversight.

I concluded my assignment as Pastor of Good Hope AME Church on Wednesday, September 20, 1966, when I made my pastoral report to the West Florida Annual Conference. A delegate from the Good Hope congregation stood with me as I reported the number of converts, baptisms, new members, marriages, deaths, the results of our stewardship efforts, the renovations, and the sense of hope and optimism that was now present in the church. The delegate made a strong appeal that the bishop reassign me to serve the church for another year. We then returned to our seats. As the delegate and I walked to our seats, the Bishop informed the Annual Conference,

"Reverend Proctor has requested a transfer to the First Episcopal District and a leave of absence from pastoral responsibilities. He has accepted a position as the Associate Executive Director of the New York State Council of Churches. I wish him God speed." With those words, a hush came over the conference. At the close of the morning session, tired of answering questions about my new position, I left the Annual Conference, drove to Delray Beach to inform The Reverend John Edwards of my decision, put our house on the real estate market and departed for Albion, NY after briefly visiting my in-laws for a couple of days.

CHAPTER 12

A NEW PARADIGM OF MINISTRY

We, my wife and nine-year-old son, arrived in Albion, NY on Saturday afternoon, September 30 at approximately 3:00 o'clock amidst falling snow. Arriving in New York from Florida to a thirty-five-degree temperature was quite an adjustment to make. We reported to the home of a Universality Unitarian minister's residence who lived in a three-story house large enough to accommodate a football team. The following day we joined our hosts for worship. However, we were eager for the stores to open on Monday morning to purchase winter clothing for the three of us.

October 1, 1966, I began a major paradigm shift in my ministry. Instead of serving as pastor for a specific congregation located at a particular address, I now was the pastor for a certain group of individuals, seasonal farm workers, their families and growers, in two counties. Before I could get started I had to secure a place to live, enroll our son in school, and do all the things necessary when moving into a new community.

Within fifteen days after arriving in this new community, this time as residents, we had purchased a new home in the center of the village of Albion, NY, one block south of the County Courthouse. This home buying experience was exhibit "A" in institutional racism. The sponsoring committee, though well intentioned, had planned for us to live three miles south of Albion and approximately fourteen miles north of Batavia in a rented farm house. The committee thought this farm house was ideally situated between the two largest towns. They did not consult me, but made the mistake of planning for me, rather than plan with me. I refused to accept their living arrangements. So, the first fifteen days were spent finding a suitable home in which to live. It took a few days of meeting different realtors to discover why the sponsoring committee had chosen a rural farm house for us to live. There was a built-in bias, better known as institutional racism. We were black; therefore, realtors did not show us rental properties nor for sale properties in some neighborhoods.

On October 10, 1966, as I was walking, one block from where we were living in the manse of the Universalist Unitarian church, I saw a "for sale" sign. I rushed to the nearest phone and called the realtor. We were shown the house and made a purchase offer. The attorney for the sellers did everything legally possible to prevent the sale. He finally added a clause to the proposed sale agreement, "The buyer must be able to close within ten days." This was highly unusual. Most times there is at least a thirty to ninety day closing period.

I photo copied the document and shared my experience with the Chairman of the sponsoring committee, a Cornell University, Ph. D. graduate and one of the largest apple growers in western New York. He shook his head and said, referring to the lawyer for the seller, "I knew he was conservative, but I didn't know he was a son of a bitch."

The sponsoring committee was a broad cross section of community leaders in Albion-Orleans County and Batavia-Genesee County New York. Members of my sponsoring committee, who were all white, except one, thought they should decide where my family and I should live. This was unacceptable to me and my refusal to allow others to make decision for me is a part of being a mature individual.

This initial experience also taught me a lesson about the differences in racism in the north and in the south. In the north, some whites gave lip service to Martin Luther Kings' work for human dignity and equality but opposed it in their own communities. Despite the ten-day clause added to the purchase offer by the seller's attorney, we had money transferred from our bank in Florida and purchased the house at 115 South First Street, Albion, NY.

It didn't take long for me to learn that I was the only African American professional living in the entire village of Albion. There was one African American woman who worked in the Orleans County courthouse as a stenographer. She lived in Buffalo and commuted to Albion on Sunday nights and back to Buffalo on Friday afternoons.

Some teachers in the public school had their built-in biases as well. I recall scheduling a parent-teacher conference to ascertain how, we as parents, could be supportive of our son's educational growth and development. We went to meet his teachers and demonstrated our willingness to become involved in the overall work of the school.

The teacher's bias was shown immediately after I introduced myself. She said, "Mr. Proctor, I am glad to meet you. Your son is one of the smartest 'colored' children in my class."

To which I replied, "I am surprised to learn that you measure smartness based on color. I am here to explore ways we can work together to help him develop to his maximum potential."

There was a long pause then nervous fidgeting to find my son's progress folder.

A few days later, our son came home from school crying. When we inquired what was wrong, he told us that one of his classmates had a birthday party last night and everyone in the class had been invited except him. I wrote the teacher a note with a copy to the principal to explain the devastating effect of allowing invitations to be distributed in class and one child was excluded. I also asked permission for our son to distribute invitations to the teacher and all the children to attend a forty-five minute "hot dog and punch party" at our home, the following Sunday afternoon. The teacher, ten children and eleven parents came to the party. After that event ended our son was included in most of the activities of his class.

Five years later as a freshman, our son and another boy were involved in a fist fight. Our son was expelled from school for three days. The other boy was not expelled. The father of the other boy called me that evening to discuss the incident. We both concluded that this was petty childish play that was being blown out of proportion by the dean of boys with the support of the high school principal. We called the principal at home that night and demanded a meeting the next morning. We all gathered in the principal's office and listened to the boys tell what had happened. Then we heard from the dean of boys and the principal. There was no discrepancy in the account each person gave.

What could not be explained, why our son was expelled for three days, and the other boy was not sanctioned at all for the same offense. I then asked the principal, "Is the reason my son is expelled because he is black?" The principal did not answer my question but gave a long rambling explanation about the code of student conduct. The father of the other boy stated, "If his son is expelled you have got to expel my son and I don't think you are prepared to do that." With that statement, the principal stated, "I'll write an excuse for these two students for being late to their first period class." Our sons left for class together and their friendship deepened because of the mutual respect of their fathers.

The man I met in the principal office of Albion High School and I became close friends. He had listened to me make presentations at a Rotary Club meeting and in his local church. He later told me that he had often dismissed ideas about individual and institutional racism. He had not fully understood how governmental and other social systems were structured against the "other," the "outsider." Mr. Jones, I will call him, became a strong supporter and gave permission for me to share this story in appropriate settings in my work in the two counties. During later conversations, he surmised that there were some individuals in positions of authority in Orleans and Genesee Counties who vehemently opposed the ministry in which I was involved but the only way they could show it was by the way they acted toward our son.

Shortly after this incident, I began to hear similar stories from other African American families. Two specific incidents in the Medina Central School district required investigation. A parent reported his son had been administered corporal punishment which was highly unusual at that time in New York state public schools. Several parents reported that their children had to watch a film about "Little Black Sambo" in a 10th grade social studies class. The film was based on Helen Banner's title of the same subject. The film depicted African

Americans in the most ignorant, deplorable, dehumanizing ways imaginable. It was reported that the white children laughed while the black children held their heads down in embarrassment.

After we did the research, gathered the facts, identified the teachers involved in each of these incidents, we shared our finding with my board of directors, one of whom was a history teacher in the Medina Central High School and a staunch supporter of our work. In this instance, however, he demurred. He made excuses for the faculty members in his school.

I scheduled a conference with the principal of the high school. The parents of the four black children involved told their story to the principal. Of course, he supported the teachers. We then wrote a letter to the superintendent of the Medina Central School District, requesting to be placed on the next School Board meeting agenda. We released a copy of the letter to the Buffalo Evening news paper. On the night of the School Board meeting; a cold, snowy, February night, my wife and I arrived to find the attendance was so large that the meeting had to be moved from the conference room in the high school library to the high school auditorium. Dairy farmers, apple and cherry growers, members of the Rotary and Kiwanians clubs, the Medina Chief of police, pastors and people from all walks of life attended the meeting. They were there to see me fall flat on my face.

By this time in my work, I was not a stranger. Everyone knew James Proctor. My picture had appeared in local and regional newspapers across western New York. When my wife and I arrived, we were met in the parking lot by Medina Chief of police and escorted to the front of the auditorium. The Chair of the School Board immediately suspended the other items on the agenda and called "Reverend Proctor to address the Board."

I slowly walked to the podium, gave the Board chair, each board member and the press a copy of my prepared statement.

My statement summarized our investigation of the two incidents, of our meetings with parents, students, the principal, and a copy of my letter to the superintendent, and reaffirmed the results of our investigation. A summary of our findings was:

- Interviews with parent, students, teachers and the principal confirmed that corporal punishment had been administered to an African American male student in violation of school policy.

- A film entitled "Little Black Sambo" had been shown to a 10th grade social studies class. The film depicted African Americans in degrading, dehumanizing, animalistic ways. The Caucasians saw the movie as hilarious, African American children saw the film as demeaning and humiliating.

In as much as the principal had not taken any actions to reprimand the offending teachers involved, I requested the Medina Central School District Board of Instruction take immediate steps to sanction the principal and teachers for this offensive, insensitive behavior toward its African American students. In addition, we demanded that African Americans be employed at every personnel level in the Medina Central District School system. The third demand was to set a time line of twelve months to implement these recommendations.

When I finished addressing the Board of Instruction, there were murmurings of disbelief. The principal was then called to rebuff my statement of findings. He admitted that after I had reported the two incidents identified above, his inquiry confirmed my report. He then reported to the members of the School Board that he was "making plans" to implement sensitivity training for all school personnel within the next sixty days. After some discussion the Board directed the principal to take appropriate steps immediately to ensure that all school personnel follow the approved guidelines for disciplining all students. Moreover, the Board admonished the principal "to take immediate steps to ensure that curriculum materials used in all classes be appropriate for all students." The chair of the Board informed the principal, "The Board will meet in executive session at the close of this regular meeting to decide what action should be taken against you." When the meeting was over the Medina Chief of police escorted my wife and me to our car.

The next morning the Medina Journal newspaper's lead article was about the overflow crowd that attended the School Board meeting and "Genesee-Orleans Ministry of Concern demands changes in the way students are disciplined." There was no mention of the hiring demands, nothing was included about the showing of "Little Black Sambo" film in my presentation before the School Board. The metropolitan newspaper, The Buffalo Evening News printed the entire statement and described the disappointment of some of the School Board members and a few residents who were interviewed by the reporter.

Our work became increasingly more challenging as we uncovered bias and institutional racism in other areas of community life. The health care delivery system, *Farmers Home Administration Agency* and in the housing area. To seek relief, we worked with people of good will to provide these services. In the health care area, we worked with the University of Rochester Medical School to provide health clinic at the Albion Hospital three evening per week. This was beneficial to the seasonal farm workers, the local hospital, and it provided excellent learning opportunities for doctors and nurses at the medical school.

The Orleans County Farmers and Home Administration had never made a loan to an African American family. Through our efforts, we created a rural self-help housing corporation and built houses for those increasing number of former seasonal agriculture workers who were settling in Orleans and Genesee counties as permeant citizens.

We also fought the discriminatory practices in rental housing. Although New York State had, at that time, one of the nation's most liberal housing discrimination statues in the country. It was often ignored in villages and rural communities. The practice of advertising a property for rent and when a black couple show up to rent it, they were told the property had been rented. A white person appears within an hour later and the place is available to be rented.

We filed a housing discrimination law suit against a politically well-connected individual in Genesee County and discovered the attorney on our Board of Directors had written a character reference for the property owner to the judge handling the case. In making my monthly report to the Board, I ended my report by submitting by resignation, stating I could no longer work for an agency and risk the safety of my family and my life when some members on the Board of Directors were working to perpetuate a system that violated the dignity of some human being. Moreover, I stated, we were working within the law to build bridges of understanding; and seek justice for those members in our communities who were the least, left out, the voiceless and those living on the out-skirts of society. Our mission was to work to ensure that the poorest among us had equal access to "justice and liberty for all."

There was absolute silence. The chair of the Board of Directors of the Genesee-Orleans Ministry of Concern said, "I am sure no one on this Board would write a letter opposing the very action that we had authorized you to take." Finally, the attorney member of the board who had written the letter spoke up and said, "I wrote the letter. I have known XYZ since high school days, he is a good man. I believe he should be able to rent his property to whoever he wants." After another long silence, a motion was made: "To support the action of our director and the Chair be authorized to send a letter to the court informing the judge of the decision of the Genesee-Orleans Ministry of Concern." The motion carried on a six to one vote. The board member who had written the letter in support of the property owner voted against the motion, and immediately resigned as a board member. His resignation was accepted, and he left the room immediately.

This was an extremely tense meeting. However, the work for justice is never easy. To be effective one must take a stand for those who cannot stand for themselves. Had the vote gone the other way, I was prepared to leave the agency rather than go along to get along. To have done otherwise would have, in my opinion, betrayed the gospel of Jesus Christ and the historic tradition of the African Methodist Episcopal Church of which I am an ordained elder. The focus of Jesus' ministry was always toward the poor, the stranger, the other, those excluded from community for ungodly reasons. At this crucial time, I could do no less.

For the most part, my work was divided into two major cycles; the first cycle dealt with the ministry to seasonal agriculture workers and their families. The intense period was from June 15 to October 15 when a large influx of workers arrived to harvest tomatoes, cherries and then the apples. For this phase of the work, I recruited college students from State University New York, Brockport, University of Rochester, Genesee Community College, senior high school students, as well as members of various church women groups in the community.

We would begin each new season with a day-long training session followed by periodic training sessions throughout the season. The cadre of volunteers were then divided into teams, each with a team leader. For the most part, we did not assign local volunteers to work in the same community where they lived. We thought it would be very difficult for the son or daughter of a farmer to report a housing code violation on their dad's farm. It was the team's leader responsibility among other things to organize the activities for his/ her team, conduct meaningful educational and recreational activities for the children of seasonal agricultural workers, file a daily report that included: a summary of the day's activities, referrals of unsolved problems, needed resources, housing violations, and prepare a statistical reports summarizing the day's activities including miles traveled, etc.

The second major phase of our work, typically November through May, involved a ministry to the increasing number of persons leaving the migrant stream for permanent year-round work in western New York state. The type of services needed for those individuals and families were different and increasingly challenging. The types of services ranged from literacy, budgeting, transportation, healthcare, daycare for children, housing, etc. We were able to meet those demands by securing resident churches to sponsor families and/or individuals.

During this period, we pressured the Farmers Home Administration to loan money to build houses for those families who were now gainfully employed in non-seasonal agriculture work. As mentioned earlier in this book, the Framers Home Administration agency had never made a loan to an African American. The Genesee-Orleans Ministry of Concern, under my leadership was able to organize a Rural Self-Help Housing Corporation in the two counties. Members covenant to work on each other's house thereby avoiding 85-90% of the labor cost. Our agency employed a building contractor who supervised the construction process. The home owner only paid for some of the highly technical electric and pluming work. In 1967-68, we were able to build quality houses using "sweat equity" (families building their own houses) for less than $20,000 in Genesee and Orleans counties.

To experience the change in a family's life who lived in a migrant camp three yeas earlier and now live in their own home that they built was a transformative experience. These individuals and families became ambassadors for our work. They were effective spokespersons for our ministry. When these new home owners told their story, they were believed.

My work with this agency brought with it a lot of publicity. There were times when it worked against me, and at times it worked for me. Every local law enforcement officer in western New York knew me. Some were friends, and some were foes. My life and that of my family were like living in a glass house. One local police officer in the village of Albion, where I live, once told me, "Mr. Proctor, anything you do not want known, do not talk about it on the phone." I thanked him and conducted many private conversations walking, or in the homes of others. I also learned how to make statements about one thing when we would do something altogether different.

On April 3, 1968 when Dr. Martin Luther King, Jr. was assassinated, I had made a presentation in a Presbyterian church approximately twenty miles from my home. I was stopped three times; before I arrived home, once by a New York State Highway Trooper, once each by a Genesee County sheriff and an Albion police officer. Each one of them asked to see my driver's license, automobile registration and proof of insurance. When I inquired, "Why did you stop me?" Each one gave a different answer. One said I was driving too slowly, another said I was driving too fast and the third one said, I want to make sure that you are alright.

This publicity also meant that I was recruited to do graduate work at *Colgate Rochester Crozier Divinity School* in Rochester, NY and the School of Social Work, State University of New York at Buffalo. In September of 1969, I was awarded a National Institute of Mental Health Fellowship and enrolled in the School of Social Work. I concentrated in Community Organization and Mental Health Evaluation. I completed the coursework requirements for the Master of Social Work degree within eighteen months. During the year and a half, I was in school, I served as a consultant to the Genesee-Orleans Ministry of Concern.

CHAPTER 13

A MINISTRY TO THOSE WITH HIDDEN PAIN

———◆———

Rarely do we think of people who are working in helping professions and those who are mentally ill as needing a minister. But there are instances in the New Testament where Jesus ministered to both the haves and the have nots. Two examples are: "A Jewish leader asked Jesus, 'Good Teacher,' what must I do to receive eternal life?" (Luke 18:18) Matthew 19:16 and Mark 10:17 describe this man as being a rich young man. This is an example of Jesus ministering to the wealthy and well connected. However, the overwhelming majority of Jesus' ministry was devoted to the poor, the sick, the outcast and those excluded from good things of life. I consider the next phase of my ministry primarily directed to the economically disadvantaged but not exclusively. Some of my work changed the lives of those who were a part of the in crowd, whose pains were masked by substance abuse and other addicting, debilitating habits.

On July 1, 1971, I was appointed the Administrator of the Mental Health Department, Anthony L. Jordan Health Center, Rochester, NY. Jordan Health Center was one of the first Health Maintenance

Organization (HMO) established in western New York. There were 205 interdisciplinary staff members consisting of dentists, nurses, physicians, psychologists, social workers, administrators, and a variety of para- professionals.

I inherited a staff that consisted of a psychiatrist, a psychologist a psychiatric nurse, a social worker and four community health assistants. The previous year the per unit of services in Jordan Mental Health Department was 100% higher than the per unit of service in Monroe county. The health center director stated concisely and forcefully that I had one year to get the cost of services to reflect the cost of mental service in the county. I indicated that this seemed to be a very unreasonable stipulation. Then, I requested a 15% salary increase if I met his target goal. After some give and take, we mutually agreed, if I met the goal, I would receive a 10% salary increase on June 30, 1972. On the other hand, if I did not reach the goal, my probationary status would be extended six months. We both signed a memorandum of understanding and it was placed in my personnel file.

My first week at the Jordan Health Center was spent reading the minutes of every staff meeting, carefully searching staff work attendance records, staff /patient therapeutic appointment records, staff broken appointment records, salaries of the various staff members, etc.

Midway through the first week, I informed everyone that I was providing lunch, during the regular lunch time on day five; and requested every staff member to attend. Two community health assistants and the psychologist did not attend. That afternoon a personal letter was placed in their mail box and a copy was mailed to their residence demanding a meeting in my office at a specified date and time. Each of the community health assistants came in angry, with a negative attitude. One of them, I'll call Ms. Brown informed me immediately, "I don't have time to talk with you, I need to see my patients." The psychologist was more tactful in expressing his disapproval of a Social Worker and a Black man calling him in.

Calmly, during my initial meeting with each of them, I reviewed their attendance records, the number of broken patient appointments, the dates and times of the broken appointments, and their performance evaluations for the last two years. They were surprised that I had taken the time to do the research and present the information in a professional manner. I indicated how much I wanted them to help make our unit the best in the county. I never lost my focus on what I was hired to do; provide quality mental health services at a rate that was comparable to other delivery systems in the county. Their anger did not affect my mission and my professionalism.

The psychologist recognized that this was a new paradigm shift. This was about performance, professionalism, and accountability. It was not about degrees or race or anything else. It was about providing excellent mental health services and doing what we both had been employed to do. We became personal and professional allies. The two community health assistants, both of whom were substances abusers, were terminated for cause.

The Jordan Health Center was in an economically depressed, diverse area of the city. Many of the people who made appointments on Mondays and Fridays did not keep them. Some low socio-economic people would start abusing substances on Friday and would carry over to Mondays. Most of the broken appointments were on Mondays and Fridays. This discovery by me in the first few days on the job made a big impact in reducing the per unit of cost of mental health services. So, we started giving staff members days off on Mondays and Fridays or reducing the numbers of work hours on those two days. Also, another strategy we employed was to do group therapy instead of individual therapy sessions. The psychiatrist role became that of the medication provider and consultant to the other professionals on staff. By month ten we had met our goal; instead of the per unit cost for mental health service in the Jordan Health Center costing $110 per visit it was down to $56 per unit of service. I met the goal set by the center's director; and on the anniversary of my hiring I received a ten per cent salary increase. This was another high moment! I had demonstrated again, the African American male, who by some standards was not supposed to attend high school could successfully compete with anyone. Again, I had successfully crossed the river.

The next three years were exciting. I was riding high. My wife and I were growing closer and our son was enjoying his life in high school in Rochester, NY as just another student and not as the son of the advocate for justice in a rural, extremely conservative community.

1974 was a pivotal year for me. It was a time when many agencies and organizations were trying to be racially diverse. I was competent, highly respected and recruited for positions in various human service organizations. Our son graduated high school and my wife and I were empty nesters. I had demonstrated to myself that I possessed the skills to go "over the river" and manage a highly educated, diverse group of individuals. I had also demonstrated that one's professional discipline did not necessarily determine one's competence. I had made friends through my networking abilities in professional associations, religious circles, graduate educational institutions and mental health agencies. Moreover, I had become nationally certified through the National Association of Social Work.

This also, for me, was a time of reflection and intense internal examination. However, I thought the next career move needed to be very strategic. I was pulled in two different directions. The pull of the pastoral ministry was ever present and yet the pull to work in a multicultural secular agency provided a challenge that was hard to overlook.

One day as I was reading one of the many professional journals that came to our office, I read an article about the University of North Carolina, School of Medicine Community Psychiatry Department offering fellowships to practitioners and educators in mental health. The opportunity to be associated with William Hollis, M. D. in a year-long educational endeavor was inviting, and it would give me the time for farther reflection.

Dr. Hollis advocated, as I did, the most effective mental health interventions are usually provided in one's natural environment, home, and community. Rarely should patients be institutionalized in psychiatric facilities in distant communities, and never for long periods of time. The article was inviting persons to apply for a fellowship to work and learn in a multi-disciplinary setting with physicians, psychologists, Social workers and Nurses who were interested in increasing their knowledge, improving their skills and enhancing their competencies in the practice and delivery of mental health services. The article captured my attention immediately. I shared it with my wife and we both started imagining what a year of study would do for me, and how being away from snowy, cold upper New York state weather would be a big boost for both of us. We mutually agreed that I should apply. I shared the article with my supervisor and received his blessings to apply. He thought it would enhance the Centers standing when applying for grants, and it would improve our effectiveness and efficiency in delivering services to an underserved, economically depressed community. I applied and was accepted. August 1,1974, I joined a cohort of six other individuals: two social workers, one an associate professor of nursing, one psychologist, one public health administrator and two psychiatrics.

Some of the members of this group used this year to research various area of interest and sharpen their skills in that area. I used the year to strengthen my knowledge and improve my skills around managing, staffing and evaluating community mental health centers.

In my role as a fellow, I had the opportunity to travel throughout the state of North Carolina evaluating community mental health centers and serve on a multi-discipline community mental health certification team. In addition, the community psychiatry department, University of North Carolina did several multi-disciplinary conferences and workshops throughout the year. Because of my expertise and hands-on experience in administration, I was often asked to participate in several of these educational activities. I made a presentation in Chapel Hill, NC advocating that social workers who were adequately trained, nurtured and supported could do an effective job of evaluating community mental centers. At the close of my presentation, a social work professor from Florida State University approached and invited me to lunch. I was gracious in declining his invitation; however, I had planned lunch with my wife that day and offered to join him for dinner.

We met for dinner and to my surprise Dr. Harris Goldstein, professor of social work at Florida State almost knew more about me than I did. My bio was in the conference bulletin, but he knew a lot more about my background. He knew I had two brothers living in Tallahassee, FL. He knew of my work with the New York State Council of Churches, and my work at the Anthony L. Jordan Health Center in Rochester, NY.

After sharing much of my professional history with me, Dr. Goldstein informed that he had received a National Institute of Mental Health grant to train social workers to do program evaluation for community mental health centers. He then invited me to make the same presentation to the faculty in the School of Social Work at Florida State University. I agreed and visited FSU in February 1975. I was well received and was offered a teaching position as Assistant Professor in the School of Social Work. With a solid job offer in hand, and a strong desire to return to Florida I had some loose ends to tie up.

Among the things I had to do was inform my superior at the Jordan Health Center that I was not returning and negotiate the best way to avoid financial pain. After considerable negotiation, we agreed that I would repay the Center for my health insurance cost for the year. I would then be released from my contract with the Jordan Health Center.

Once I returned to North Carolina, I did not immediately complete the application. This was not done out of malice, but when I left Florida in 1966 Florida State University was a hostile place for African Americans. I made it clear to Dr. Goldstein that I desired to work in an institution that supported its faculty's involvement in the life of the community. I refused to fill out the application until I visited the campus again to meet with the dean and discuss these concerns. I was invited back to FSU and I met with the dean a second time and other stakeholders in the school and shared my philosophy about teaching and its application to life's current conditions. I was assured that if I fulfilled my responsibilities to the university in a highly effective manner; and not bring disgrace on the university, nor its faculty members, I would be supported and encouraged to become actively involved in the life of the community. With this assurance, I joined the faculty on July 1, 1975.

CHAPTER 14

A MINISTRY OF HIGHER EDUCATION

———◆———

Within fifteen months after joining the faculty, I was elected president of the Tallahassee Branch of the National Association for the Advancement of Colored People (NAACP). My election made the papers in the local Tallahassee Democrat newspaper and the campus newspaper. Some of my colleagues predicted that I would be fired within two years. I was meticulous in documenting my office hours and accepted more advisees than required, and I was always prompt for meetings. I volunteered to do extra work for the school. I prepared and taught my classes well; receiving excellent student evaluations and above average evaluation from my chair and dean each year.

In addition to my work in the wider community, I became very active in the internal affairs of the school of social work. I volunteered to serve on two important committees in the school: hiring, promotion and tenure, and the admissions committee. These two committees basically decided the makeup of the school's population; its faculty and its student body. The committee on hiring, promotion and tenure, for the most part, determined who was invited for personal interview with members of the committee, who was asked to make presentations and who was recommended to the dean for hiring, promotion and tenure. This committee played a central role in who was promoted and tenured. Prior to my serving on this committee, only tenured, associates and full professors made all the recommendations regarding hiring, promotion, retention and tenured. The same was true with the admissions committee. The student body looked like the members of the admissions committee. I do not mean to suggest that the members of the faculty of the school of social work were prejudiced or racist. I am suggesting that they, for the most part, valued and gave credit to experiences with which they were familiar. And this was true when recommending members for the faculty and recommending students for admission to the school.

This was a hard sell for the first two years of my employment. I recall one faculty meeting during the spring of my second year when a male, tenured professor inquired, "Who is the faculty advisor for Jane Doe?"

I replied, "I am her advisor, is there a problem?"

His response was starling. "Ask her," he said, "Why is she always hanging on to men on this campus?"

I promised to ask the student during our next teacher student conference. I then noted that I had seen quite a bit of male-female close student interaction, but I wonder, "if your concern is because this student is white, and the male student is black?"

He did not respond to my question. During the next faculty meeting, I reported the student's response. She expressed disappointment that a professor in the school of social of work would inquire about her right to choose the friends with whom she associated. After that meeting, we were able to seriously engage each other around issues of individual and institutional racism and diversity in the school of social work and in the community.

During the entire time I served on the faculty at Florida State University, I also served as pastor of small member AME churches in Gadsden County, approximately twenty minutes from the Florida State University campus. In 1978, Bishop Samuel Morris visited the congregation I was serving and was significantly impressed with my leadership. He requested that I prepare to assume a full-time pastorate in the next Annual Conference. He also informed me that the appointment would necessitate relocating from the Tallahassee community.

The four years employment at FSU gave me an opportunity to challenge many of the unconscious biases we hold. It also helped to significantly increase the number of minority students in the school of social work and demonstrated one did not have to be a tenured professor to ask questions and evaluate one's professional value to an institution. Moreover, position on the faculty and work in the community brought publicity and visibility to FSU school of social work. I include this phase of my life as a ministry of higher education.

CHAPTER 15

THE PASTORAL MINISTRY

———◆———

On October 18, 1979, I was assigned to the pastorate of Hurst Chapel African Methodist Episcopal Church in Winter Haven, Fl. My employment with FSU officially ended December 31, 1979. To accept that pastoral appointment involved some significant financial sacrifices for my wife and me. Together, our earnings dropped $48,000. At FSU, we were living in our newly acquired four-bed room, two car garage home. When we arrived in Winter Haven the house provided for the pastor was in a crime ridden, deteriorated area of the city.

I willingly accepted the offer to assume a full-time pastorate in the AME Church because I felt this ultimately was my calling, my vocation. The previous positions in New York, by the help of God had allowed us to accumulate enough resources not be destitute. Despite this, the adjustment was difficult. I literally became depressed. The first month after we moved to our new assignment, life for me seemed dark and hopeless. For the first time, I experienced real depression. It was difficult for me to concentrate, sleep, prepare sermons and tackle the many pressing issues confronting the pastor of this congregation at that time.

At that time, for the most part, African Americans lived in the northwest and southeast sections of the city. Everyone knew everyone and I as the new pastor needed to be at my best. I was faking it. I was far from my best. By the third week in January 1980, I had perfected the art of disguise. I would arise early every morning and walk and pray. One morning, before dawn as I walked and prayed, it seemed as if I heard a loud audible voice. It said, "I promise to take care of you." I stopped and looked around but did not see anyone. I completed the walk and returned home. My sense of darkness, doubt, depression and discontent vanished. I was back to my old self feeling I was not alone. I was doing the will of God.

About 10:00 o'clock that morning, the phone rang. Someone on the other end asked, "Pastor do you and Mrs. Proctor eat fish?"

I replied with a reassuring "Yes!"

Within an hour several freshly caught and cleaned fish were brought to our home. Later that same day another parishioner called my wife to inquire if we ate steaks. When she replied with the assurance that we eat steaks, but our budget did not allow for steaks. Again, she was told that our menu could afford steaks in the future. From that day forward, for the next two years, I doubt if we spent

$200.00 on groceries. God did open people's hearts and took care of us.

For the first two months of my pastorate in Winter Haven, I conducted worship services and held the business meetings to manage the temporal affairs of the church, performed pastoral care functions such as visiting the institutionalized and ill members of the church. The word traveled throughout the congregation that our new pastor is concerned about all the members, even those who are unable to attend church. I listened intently to each person I encountered. In different ways, two similar themes kept coming up: there was a lack of transparency in the financial management of the church and rumors about the sudden departure of the previous pastor, whose tenure was only five- or six-months duration.

The first concern was one that I could rectify. Fiscal management had been a strong point in my positions at the Jordan Health Center, the New York State Council of Churches and my first pastorate at Good Hope more than a decade ago. I set out to identify nine individuals who I, and others suggested as people of unquestioned integrity. In most congregations, there are persons who are gifted, and if trained, nurtured, supported and held accountable will perform the tasks of the church in a highly effective manner. These nine individuals were chosen; three from the Board of Stewards, three from the Board of Trustees and three from the congregation at large. They were organized as the Commission on Stewardship and Finance. Their specific function was to assist the pastor in planning, implementing and managing the financial resources of the church. This commission was also charged with the responsibility to inform the members, by the 10th of every month in writing: the receipts for the month, who contributed, the expenses and who was paid. By June 30, 1980, the level of giving had increased 51% over the previous six months. The rumors about the sudden departure of my predecessor remained rumors and I never addressed them.

By October of that same year the Board of Trustees recommended to the Official Board, the Trustees be authorized to purchase a new parsonage in a "safe residential area for the pastor to live." The motion was approved by the Official Board and submitted to the Church Conference for congregational approval. The motion was overwhelmingly approved by the congregation and within short order a house was purchased, and we moved into a new parsonage in a residential area of the city. Within two years the membership was on the rebound. There was new growth, new ministries and a new sense of pride by the members. Two years and three months after my initial appointment to Hurst Chapel, I was assigned to the pastorate of Saint Paul African Methodist Episcopal Church in Jacksonville, FL.

My tenure at Saint Paul began January 1, 1982. This assignment signaled that I was among an elite class of pastors in the entire international body of the African Methodist Episcopal Church. I was thrilled to be assigned to the largest AME church in Jacksonville with a membership of over 1400 members. On my arrival, I was welcomed by three Trustees and one Steward which was unusual.

It had been my experience in previous churches to be welcomed by members of the Board of Stewards, whose duty it is to help manage the spiritual and fiscal affairs of each local congregation. The Trustees, on the other hand are responsible for managing the temporal affairs of the church: property, buildings, vehicles, equipment, etc. During this approximately hour-long meeting, I was shown the sanctuary, which was a huge transept style, brick building that required walking up thirteen steps to reach the worship area. Upon entering that sacred space, I immediately knelt at the altar and gave thanks to God for the opportunity to serve the people of this city.

After touring the physical property four things immediately stood out. First, the number of steps to get to the worship space. Second, the location of the pastor's study. Third was the lack of classrooms in the facility. And fourth, the absence of off-street parking spaces.

The final stop on my initial tour was the parsonage. It was a three-bedroom house adjacent to the church's property. The parsonage was not a welcoming place to live. In short, it was unlivable. When I saw it my mind instantly fell on my wife. She would be the person spending many hours in this place each day. My initial visit with the four men ended with two questions: The first, are there members of the congregation who are sick and need the attention of the pastor? The second questions I asked, please direct me to good hotel where I can spend some time until we can make the parsonage livable? The first question demonstrated my concern for the sick and shut-in members. My second question demonstrated a concern for my family. As I walked to my car, one of the trustees handed me a folder and said, "This folder contains the budget for the next twelve months." I accepted the folder and asked, if he was the chair pro tem of the Commission on Stewardship and Finance? (In the AME church, the pastor is chair of the Commission on Stewardship and Finance.) He replied "No, but I thought this would be helpful to our new pastor." I put the folder in my brief case, the budget was not the farthest thing from my mind at that time.

The day was Sunday, my first worship experience at this congregation. The order of service for my initial worship experience at Saint Paul was planned before I arrived. It was somewhat different than the services I had been accustomed to in my previous assignments. That initial worship service was more formal; with introits, hymns, spirituals, choral responses and anthems. My first sermon was based on the story of Moses sending out twelve spies to do a reconnaissance of the land which God was giving the Hebrew people. The passage is in Numbers 13:1-33. The sermon was intended to do three things: First, I introduced myself and admitted that they and I were grieving. We, congregants and pastor, were grieving the loss of familiar faces. They were grieving the loss of the pastor who had served them for eighteen years. They saw standing before them a stranger and heard a strange voice, who was also grieving the love and support of a loving congregation whom I had served for more than two years. By acknowledging the loss of their former pastor, I tapped into what some of the parishioners were feeling and gave them permission to acknowledge it. The second thing the sermon was intended to do was to articulate the challenge of entering new paradigms of ministry together. I acknowledged that our new beginning would not be easy.

This part of the sermon retold how leaders were chosen from the various groups, families to participate in this reconnaissance effort. I promised in my ministry, of shepherding God's people at Saint Paul A. M. E. Church to involve representatives from the various groups to help determine our journey ahead. Moreover, this part of the sermon reminded the congregants that the twelve spies Moses sent to thoroughly investigate what the conditions were like; basically, they all saw the same things. All the spies agreed, the land was fertile and productive, the fruit was huge and plentiful; and the cities were large *and well-fortified. The King James version of scripture says, "The land flows with milk and honey."* In addition, the spies reported that giants lived in the land and we looked like grasshoppers in their sight. Most of the men, 80 percent of those ten of the twelve, sent to check out the conditions in the land concluded, we cannot take the land. We cannot possess it, we cannot go forward. When that report was made to the congregation of Israel the members panicked and became frightened. Then Caleb, an extremely small minority, silenced the people who were complaining against Moses, their pastor, and said: *"We should attack now and take the land; we are strong enough to conquer it" (Numbers 13:30).*

The third point my initial sermon was intended to make was to demonstrate to the congregants that people of every age have doubters who only see opposition, and never see the opportunities God has made for us. The majority usually see the size of the opposing forces, without seeing the gifts, knowledge, skills and abilities God has given God's people to accomplish God's mission in the world. The closing challenge was to acknowledge there are people in this congregation who, like the Israelites, are afraid and fearful of the journey ahead. They are afraid of the challenges of this new year and a new era of ministry in this community. They distrusted their God-given resources, skills and abilities. They mistrusted the skills and abilities of the new leader God had placed here to lead you forward.

My final challenge to the congregants on January 3, 1982, God had sent me to be their Moses. And I, like Moses, would be spending the next several weeks in recognizance and analysis. This recognizance would be led by a broad cross section of all the congregants. We, together, would identify people who want to go forward, people who are tired of wandering in the wilderness of inadequate facilities, and ineffective ministry. I reminded them, we, together, would identify the giants in this congregation who always say, "We have never done it that way." Or the other famous seven words that hamper progress, "We don't do it that way here." We, together, would identify the well-camouflaged, deeply dug-in enemies to progress. Together, let us go forward!

My message was well received by some members, based on their comments as they departed the worship service. Others shook my hand; some saying, "We really miss our pastor." I smiled and acknowledged their honesty.

Monday night, January 4, 1982, 7:00 o'clock was the scheduled time for the Official Board meeting. This is a formal meeting of the officers of each congregation. Its primary function is to plan, implement and manage the spiritual and temporal affairs of the church. It is comprised of the Stewards, Trustees, Class Leaders, Stewardesses, Chairperson of every auxiliary, board or club. The Official Board, for the uninitiated pastor, can test one's skills to conduct the business affairs of the church. I carefully prepared the agenda for this first session. Included on the agenda was an intense, intentional devotional period. The pastor, for me, is not the chief executive officer. The pastor is the shepherd; therefore, he/she must frame all that he/she does considering a shepherd/leader mentality.

As each person entered the room that night, I greeted them, and he/she received a copy of the agenda. This was a surprise to the attendees. The agenda contained the following items: Call to order, approval of agenda, devotion, election of a secretary, secretary's minutes of the last meeting, treasurer's report, the disciplinary questions regarding the spiritual conditions of the congregants, etc. and report of each groups ministry for the previous month, including money raised and balance in each group's treasury; and I asked each chairperson how long he/she had served as chair of the various groups. That first Official Board meeting revealed volumes about the spiritual and fiscal strength of the Saint Paul congregation.

First there was very little pastoral care being provided for the members. Secondly, the Christian educational ministry had no central, unifying focus. The Sunday school teachers made little effort to make the lessons interesting and relevant. That first Official Board meeting also revealed there was no centralized administrative structure. When the time came for summary reports regarding ministry from the various groups the meeting disintegrated into low level murmurings and confusion. Two chairpersons, stated, "Our group does not make reports to the Official Board." Also, I learned, one person had served as president of a group for forty-one years. One could see a congregation that was drifting. This congregation, that night, *reminded me of Jesus' ministry of whom it was said, "When he saw the crowds, he had compassion for them, because they were harassed and helpless, like sheep without a shepherd" (Matthew 9:36 NRSV).*

I left the meeting realizing that I had been assigned to a 1400-member congregation that was spiritual and fiscally bankrupt. A little more inquiring the next few days indicated, the previous pastor had been ill for the last two years, and the members had been extremely compassionate toward him, but the church suffered because of the lack of leadership. Financial records were in disarray. It was clear the church was not receiving enough money to: initiate and provide ministry, pay the pastor, operate the building, keep the utilities paid and pay the apportionments.

The financial picture was extremely bleak. The officers had borrowed money from the members to disguise the real picture. This meant no salary for the current pastor, no housing allowance, no moving allowance, etc. In addition, the parsonage was really in bad shape. It was unlivable. Therefore, I lived in a hotel for six weeks, paid the costs, and paid my moving expenses. At the end of six weeks the church was operating in the black again for the first time in two or three years. The parsonage had been refurbished. I was reimbursed for my expenses on February 15, 1982. The fact that I showed a willingness to sacrifice and ensure that others be paid first endeared me to some of the senior leaders of the church.

God blessed our ministry and the church that was fiscally and spiritually bankrupt dedicated a new $3.5 million-dollar multipurpose worship, educational and community service facility on September 1, 1991. That campus stands today as a testimony to what can happen when a group of people is led by a shepherd who loves them, is transparent in financial matters, practices a theology that God has gifted all people. My task as pastor, was to equip the members for ministry.

Another major role of my pastorate was to affirm those God given gifts, nurture those individuals, support them and hold them accountable. When pastor and people, even if they are in the minority at first, trust God wholeheartedly, God will do great things through them.

Not only did we build a magnificent facility that is a model of excellence for the African Methodist Episcopal Church. In addition to building a fine facility, we built men and women who provided holistic ministries at the local level. Six years after beginning this pastorate, one person, who had never been a delegate to the General Conference prior to pastorate rose to be president of the Lay Organization. Several of them rose to positions of leadership at the district, conference and episcopal district levels. Also, several persons who entered vocational ministry, have led and/or leading statewide activities in our denomination.

After completing the construction of the new facility, I enrolled in Drew University School of Theology and earned a Doctor of Ministry degree. My dissertation was entitled, "Planning and Implementing a Lay Pastoral Care Ministry in Saint Paul African Methodist Episcopal Church, Jacksonville, Florida." My doctoral project involved the entire congregation. My educational endeavor at this point in my career enabled me to better equip more members for ministry.

In addition to serving as pastor for Saint Paul, I was elected a delegate to the General Conference of the AME Church five times, a member of the General Board of the AME Church, Director of Christian Education for the 11th Episcopal District (Florida and the Bahama Island), Chair of the Board of Examiners for the East Conference, delegate to two World Methodist Conferences in Nairobi and Singapore. I aspired to be elected a bishop in our church 1996. I was not elected. After my unsuccessful run for the office of bishop, I returned to the people whom I loved and served them for four more years.

On November 18, 2000, I was appointed to the position of Presiding Elder in the East Florida Conference after my tenure at Saint Paul. The role of presiding elder in the African Methodist Episcopal church is an interesting one. The office requires its occupants to monitor the performance of pastors, make recommendations to the bishop for pastors to be assigned to the various churches, receive and reports the apportionments from the churches and helps establishes new congregations. He/she also examines candidates who make application to enter the ministry of the AME church. In each of my previous positions I had been cited for excellent managerial skills. In a real sense, presiding elders hold little authority over pastor's leadership. Presiding elders recommend but have little enforcement power over incompetent pastors. I do not blame the pastors with whom I worked because few of them saw the role of pastor as I did. Again, I saw the role of pastor as a shepherd, a leader, someone who influences. Many of the pastors with whom I served, saw the role of pastor as that, a cowboy/cowgirl. They would never use that term. They saw themselves as Chief Operating Officers (CEO's), as driver; and not a leader, influencer or shepherd. That is contrary to the teaching of Jesus. Who said, *"Whoever wants to be first must be last of all and servant of all" (Mark 9:35 NRSV)*. Some of the pastors were never effective as pastors. Some were excellent preachers but never developed the art of listening, empathizing and demonstrating love for the parishioners they were assigned to serve. I served my last four year of itinerant ministry in the role of presiding elder. I retired from the itinerancy in November 2004 after forty years of service.

CHAPTER 16

AFTER THE ITINERARY

———◆———

On November 5, 2004, the day of my retirement from Itinerant Ministry was a happy occasion! It was an event I had anticipated. Although, I had witnessed and or participated in the retirement services of others for at least forty times, this was different. The statements, the liturgy applied to me. It seemed as if I was the unique object of every word. I listened intently to every word Bishop McKinley Young spoke. He eloquently said:

The record of your active ministry is written. It is written in the record of God. Your church is deeply grateful for your ministry and for the care which you have exercised in faithfully fulfilling your vows of ordination. May the precious memories of your years of sacrificial service and fruitful labor be blessed and hallowed.

And now, as you yield your official responsibilities in the active ministry of the African Methodist Episcopal Church, be assured that the years that are yet to be, may be filled with good works and become the crown of all your ministry, bringing glory and honor to you and to the church. The

congregation of which you will be a member will look to you
for spiritual guidance and godly example. Your colleagues in
the ministry will continue to seek and respect your counsel.
They will annually listen for your answer to the "Roll Call"
of the Conference (The Doctrine and Discipline of the African
Methodist Episcopal Church, P. 658).

When the 2004, Annual Conference ended, I felt relieved of the responsibilities associated with Itinerant Ministry. This was the time, I thought, my wife who had made significant sacrifices for my career and I could enjoy gardening, raising Nubian goats and traveling. In anticipation of my retirement, we purchased two plots of land; one an acre and a half on which we built our house, and a five acres tract nearby, both on Bridges Road, Jacksonville, FL in an area that had previously been a dairy farm. We both (my wife and I) had grown up on farms and knew gardening and raising goats were not instant gratifying hobbies; like ministry, we had to work and wait for the harvest. However, we did not hesitate to get started.

It took time to plan, prepare the soil, plant the seeds, transplant the rose bushes and fruit trees, build the fences and construct the barn to protect the goats. But these were things we painstakingly did together. We planned together, we selected the seeds, rose bushes and fruit trees. We went together to buy our first two goats. The first two goats we purchased were pregnant females. Within two months one of them gave birth to two kids. The baby goats were healthy and vibrant, but the mother goat abandoned them. She would not allow the babies to nurse. In quick order, we bought goat milk and a nursing bottle, then we alternated bottle feeding the babies.

One morning as my wife was feeding the baby goats two vicious dogs dug under the professionally installed fence, attacked my wife as she fed the baby goat, killing the goats. My wife escaped but the goat was ripped apart. I put one dog down, and left it laying in the pasture for my neighbors who owned the vicious dogs to see. After a couple of days, the dog was eaten by vultures. We did not have any other problems from dogs. That was a sad and difficult day. That episode made me angry. We had spent one thousand seven hundred dollars to have a fence installed to protect our animals. Like David, in the Old Testament, who protected his sheep from wild animals, I thought it my moral and legal responsibility to protect my family and my property. A few months later we purchased two more female and a male goat. Within six years our herd had increased to eighteen.

We grew a variety of vegetables in our garden, far more than we could eat. We gave them to neighbors and members of our church. We grew mustards, turnips, collards, egg plants, carrots, radishes, yellow and zucchini squash, tomatoes, white potatoes, sweet potatoes, okra, peppers, cucumbers and sweet corn. Our yard is populated with pear trees, two variety of fig trees, a Japanese persimmon tree, and two varieties of grapes. The front yard was my wife's domain where each year she added a new variety of roses to her rose garden.

CHAPTER 17

OTHER MINISTRIES

The Proctors

The first few months after my retirement were times when my wife and I spent long hours together. In addition to the gardening and raising goats; we reviewed some of the economic struggles we had experienced, the lows, and we recalled some of the good times, the highs.

Some of the experiences we talked about were the time in 1955 during my senior year in college when she was pregnant, and I was depending on my GI check to buy groceries. The mail carrier came Friday August 20th and did not leave a check. We had eaten the last meal, even scraped the peanut butter jar. There was no more food in the pantry. The refrigerator was empty, nothing left.

I left home walking and the first person I met, I spoke and identified myself, saying, "I am James Proctor. I live in the next block at 2611 Delaware Street. I am a student at Florida A and M University.

I work part-time, and I am a veteran, receiving one hundred and twenty dollars ($120.00) per month. Today is the 20th and my check didn't come. We are out of food. You've got to loan me twenty dollars until my check comes!"

The stranger replied, "You are serious, aren't you?"

Before I could respond he gave me twenty dollars and then I asked for his address. We bought groceries for the weekend, my GI check came on Monday and I repaid the stranger.

We also shared an incident, after we were married when we visited her parent's home and a letter had come from a former boyfriend. Rose's mother gave me the letter and said, "She better write and tell him, she is unavailable now." We recalled and shared the exhilaration we both felt when our son was born. I reminded her of the smile on her face when we purchased our first home. The weeks and months after retirement were occasions of rediscovery and reconnecting.

This was the first time in four decades, we could decide which congregation with which we wanted to unite. We talked about the churches in Jacksonville and quickly agreed that we would not unite with the congregation we had served for nineteen years. In our opinion, although we had been away for four years, it could potentially create tension for my successor. We agreed to write the name of a church on a piece of paper and exchange papers at the breakfast table the next morning. Strangely enough, we both wrote

Greater Grant Memorial AME Church. My wife suggested that I interview the pastor to ascertain if he would feel comfortable for us to be members of the congregation. After all, Rose said, "You were his Presiding Elder until two weeks ago."

In addition, she reminded me, "You have always played a mentoring role in his life." I followed her advice, invited the pastor to breakfast at a nice restaurant and told him of our desire to become members of Greater Grant Church, but would join elsewhere if he was uncomfortable with our decision.

His face beamed with joy; saying, "I will be happy to have you and Mrs. Proctor as members of the Greater Grant Church."

Then he asked, "What do you want to do?"

"I'm retired! I want to worship in the pews with my wife, and we come to the chancellery rail together for Holy Communion. For forty years we have been on the opposite side of the chancellery rail. The only thing I would like to do is teach a Sunday School class."

The pastor paused for a moment and then said, "I need you to help me administer the Sacrament of Holy Communion. Will you help me with that service?"

I agreed to help on those occasions and reiterated that I would be seated in the pews with my wife on other occasions. The Reverend

Tony Hansberry then asked if I would lead the Justice Ministry work at Grant? With that request, my face lit up!

The next Sunday, Mrs. Proctor and I stood before the pastor and congregants and united with Greater Grant Memorial African Methodist Episcopal Church, one of the churches I had supervised as the Presiding Elder, three weeks earlier. At this stage in life, I was soaring above the clouds! We, Rose and I, were enjoying life. Our hobbies kept us busy, and they were therapeutic for me. I had made it "over the river."

As pastor Hansberry had agreed, the first responsibilities I assumed in Greater Grant was teaching one of the adult Sunday School classes. The pastor announced that Dr. Proctor will be teaching a new class in the Christian educational building, room number 5, if you are interested, you are welcome to meet him next Sunday. I was very careful and did not recruit members from any of the existing classes.

Within three weeks the class had reach its ideal size of 15 persons. For the first six or seven months the number vacillated from nine to fifteen. Some people came because a friend was enrolled, others came to see what I was like. Some learners left immediately when they discovered, I took the teaching responsibility seriously and this was not a social hour. I expected learners to be punctual, to be prepared for class each week, and to participate in the learning activities. After twelve years, the class membership has stabilized to fifteen persons. Members of the class include: a financial analyst, one former elementary school principal, four retired public-school teachers, one former nurse, one former AME pastor, a former social worker, an independent contractor, an accountant, a chemist, an executive assistant, and a bank customer service representative. Each learner brings a unique, personal story, a specific walk with God, and a different view of what it means to be a Christian.

The position as Sunday School teacher helps keep me sharp. Each week I spend five to ten hours researching, preparing and thinking of new, interesting ways to involve each member of the class. For those who are less assertive, I am quick to encourage and always find something positive to say about their contributions. It is my desire to help learners understand the Scriptures in context, and exegetically examine the passage. Then we try to ascertain what the passage is saying to us in the twenty-first century. Also, I strive to help the learners find ways to apply the lessons to daily living to build a better community. Our questions, discussions, and analyses are personal; such as What do you think? What will you do differently? How will you apply this teaching?

For me, church school study is not effective when the goal is memorization. It is effective, however, when there is a clear exegetical and hermeneutical understanding of the text, and efforts are made to apply the biblical teachings to our individual and congregational lives.

In addition to the serious study, the members of the class have bonded as a family. We genuinely care for one another. We hold two social events annually just to fellowship; one in the summer and the other during the Advent-Christmas season.

The other ministry to which I have committed myself is the Grant Memorial Justice Ministry. Injustice is so deeply ingrained in our society it is impossible for one church to make a difference in our communities Therefore, Greater Grant Memorial AME church joined with thirty-seven other interfaith racially and economically diverse congregations throughout Duval County.

I believe there are two kinds of power; money and organized people. We as African Americans are among the ninety-nine percent of Americans excluded from ninety-nine percent of the wealth. Therefore, we do not have money power. The Justice Ministry organizes its members to hold elected and appointed officials accountable to do justice for all the residents in the community; especially those who live on the periphery of society. These include economically disadvantage groups, ex-offenders, many of whom have paid their debt to society and still, by Florida statues are denied the right to vote.

I am grateful to Pastor Tony Hansberry for asking me to assume the role of coordinator of Greater Grant's Memorial AME Church's Justice Ministry. It gave me the opportunity to use organizing and leadership skills to influence others to live out their God's given responsibility as stated in the Hebrew Scriptures *"He [God] has told you, O mortal what is good; and what does the Lord require of you but to do justice, and to love kindness, and to walk humbly with your God" (Micah 6:8 NRSV).* In the Christian Scriptures, Jesus denounces the actions of the Scribes and Pharisees for their emphasis on ritualistic worship while disregarding justice. Jesus said, *"Woe to you, Scribes and Pharisees, hypocrites! For you tithe mint, dill, and cumin, and have neglected the weightier matters of the law; justice and mercy and faith. You blind guides! It is these you ought to have practiced without neglecting the others. You blind guides! You strain out a gnat but swallow a camel (Matthew 23:23-24, NRSV).*

We were able to build the foundation for a justice ministry at Greater Grant that consists of nine team leaders whose responsibility it is to recruit at least ten other members who commit to: 1) attend an annual meeting called the Nehemiah Action, 2) bring at least three other persons the annual assembly, 3) attend three other meetings throughout the year, and 4) invest at least $200.00.

To be affective, and demand constructive, long-term equitable changes in the criminal justice system, police department, and the public educational systems in Duval County, our congregation joined an umbrella organization, the Interfaith Coalition for Reconciliation and Empowerment (ICARE), a 501 C (3), not-for-profit, non-partisan organization. ICARE consists of 37, interfaith, racially and economically diverse religious congregations. Great Grant's pastor, successor to Pastor Hansberry, The Reverend Tan Moss is one of the strong leaders in the ICARE organization.

The stages of our work are divided into four distinct, but sometimes, overlapping phases: First, our justice ministry team leaders begin each year with intensive listening sessions. We listen to the problems, concerns, issues our members identify. Second, we democratically (by majority vote) choose one or more of the problems identified by the various members. Third, we do our research to find the best practices or solutions to solve the problem(s) identified by our members. Fourth, we call a big assembly, the Nehemiah Action and negotiate what we believe is an equitable solution to the problem(s). This is like the non-violent direct action made popular in the United States by Dr. Martin Luther King, Jr. in Brigham, AL and elsewhere. Dr. King wrote in his Letter from a Birmingham Jail, April 16, 1963, "In any nonviolent campaign there are four basic steps: collection of the facts to determine whether injustice exist; negotiation; self-purification; and direct action" (www.africa. penn.edu/ArticleGen/Letter_Birmingham.html).

Among the victories our justice ministry has won are the following: demanded the Duval County Public School system implement a reading curriculum that significantly improves reading for elementary school children. We forced the Jacksonville Transportation Authority to install bus hubs and direct transportation routes from the high unemployment area on the north side of the city to the south side where there were employment opportunities.

Another significant accomplishment was to compel the State Attorney and the Sheriff to stop arresting first time, nonviolent, misdemeanor juveniles and instead issue civil citations and create Neighborhood Accountability Boards to adjudicate these cases. Youth diverted to this diversionary program avoided a criminal record; the offending entity was involved in the sanction. In addition, a similar program in all middle and senior high schools has been implemented to help prevent the "school-to-prison pipeline."

We also compelled the Jacksonville Sheriff Office to implement a program for those felony who had served their prison terms and were re-entering the community. It is called the Jacksonville Reentry Center (JREC). The program is highly effective, reducing the recidivism rate by eighty percent. That is, ex-felonies who successfully completed the program did nor re-offend within a period of two years (ICARE Annual Report). Each of the programs dealing with the criminal justice system either helped prevent youth from acquiring a criminal record and help those with records to become productive citizens without proximately $385.00 to process a youth with a civil citation and $5,485.00 to arrest youth and process them through the criminal justice system. Our efforts were successful in getting a Senate Bill enacted through the Florida Legislature and signed by the governor during the 2018 legislative session.

CHAPTER 18

THE VALLEY

———◆———

A couple of years after I retired from the Itinerant Ministry, gradually, I noticed a change in my wife's behavior. Her personality changed. She became irritable, argumentative; and was not sleeping well. For the first time in her driving history she was involved in three minor auto accidents within four months.

These symptoms got worse with the passing of time. We attended Sunday School one Sunday and someone came to me and said Mrs. Proctor is outside looking for her car. I left my class and reminded her we came to church school in my car. Her car was at home.

A few weeks after that incident my wife had a scheduled 9:00 o'clock appointment with her primary care physician whose office was located only ten to twelve minutes from our home. When she had not returned by noon, I became extremely worried. Finally, she arrived at 1:00 p. m. with a strange look on her face.

Without saying anything, she immediately went to our bedroom and changed clothes. As she walked into the kitchen, I put my arms around her shoulders and asked, "How did your doctor's visit go today?"

She hesitated for a moment or two and said, "I didn't see the doctor."

I asked, "Why she did not see you?"

My wife looked at the floor and said, "I missed my turn and when I found myself I was in Georgia. I stopped at a service station and a young man showed me how to get back home."

I gave a loud vocal "Thank you Lord!" Then calmly said, "I'll take you to the doctor."

Then came the curt reply, "I don't need you to take me to the doctor."

I served her lunch and when I got a chance, I went outside and called our physician to explain what had happened. We were given an appointment for the next morning, my wife was given a cursory examination and referred to a neurologist who diagnosed her with moderate-stage of Alzheimer's disease.

Over the next several months it was painful to watch her decline. Three different medications were prescribed but the side effects to each of the medicines worsened her condition. In short, the medications caused visual and auditory hallucinations. We had to stop using the meds.

With her worsening condition, I became a full-time caregiver. One day I made a quick trip to a convenience store to get milk, when I returned she had fallen and could not get up. There was a trip to the hospital emergency room where I was questioned intently as if I were a common criminal. My wife had a broken collar bone. I got Home Health Services to come to our home to care for her. During the day she was very docile and slept for the most part. However, the health care workers went home at 5:00 p. m. every afternoon and I was left to care for her every night. She would walk from room to room inside our home. Often, she'd refuse to get in bed; therefore, I would not go to bed, afraid she would fall again or wander outside. Within three months, I had lost fifteen pounds. When I visited my primary care physician, she threatened to hospitalize me for my betterment.

However, during the valley experience, people have been supportive of us in this stage of our lives. Flowers, cards, calls, visits and words of encouragement are frequent; and from people whose life we touched years ago. In addition, our son frequently visits and gives me rest.

I tried desperately to care for my wife at home, for approximately fifteen months. My professional judgement said this is more than you can do. My pride, my sense of "what others will think" prevented me from doing what I knew in my heart of hearts I should do. There was a period when I refused to get in bed for three nights in succession because I was afraid she would fall. However, on the fourth night I fell asleep sitting beside her bed, suddenly I was awakened by a loud thump. She had fallen again. We made our way to the hospital again, arriving at 1:10 a. m. I was again interrogated. Where was I when this happened? What did I do? She finally was admitted to the hospital at 1:30 that afternoon. From there to a rehabilitation center and to a skilled nursing home.

As an African American male who grew up believing a man should be able to care for his family, I thought I could care for my wife who had sacrificed so much for me. I came to realize my thoughts were not rational. They were based on the advice I had given others many times over. My thoughts were based on what was best for my wife not me. They were based on what I assumed others would think. After all, I surmised, what will the members of Saint Paul AME church think about you. Once, I realized the decision to place her in a nursing home was best for her and for me, I agreed for her to be placed in the farthest facility from the church I had served for nineteen years and the community where I lived. I placed her in the San Jose Nursing Home, Orange Park, FL which is approximately thirty miles from where I live.

Six months passed before a member of the Board of Trustees of Saint Paul church, where I had served, call me one Thursday afternoon and said, "Rev. Proctor, I'm in your wife's room and she wants to go home." I was startled with his statement. I didn't believe anyone would be that insensitive. I simply laid the phone down with tears streaming from my eyes. The pain I felt was unbearable!

The next week about the same time this same man called again with the same words; at that time, I emphatically stated, "Do not go back to my wife's room again!"

A few months later, I transferred my wife to a five-star facility that was rated by US Report and World News magazine, at that time, as one of the *"50 Best Nursing Homes in the Country."* The facility is ten minutes from my home and I get to serve her breakfast every day.

Instead of the cross-country automobile travel we had planned, I travel daily to the nursing home to say and demonstrate my love for her. Each morning I pray with her and comfort her. This is my valley. This is my pain. Psalm 23:4 *"Even though I walk through the darkest valley, I fear no evil; for you are with me;" your rod and staff they comfort me"* has come to mean more to me now than ever before.

Approximately two and a half years after my wife was diagnosed with dementia, I was at a low point. Retirement had not been everything we had hoped for. My partner in life and ministry, the person who had sacrificed so much for me and my career was now ill. No longer were we able to see and smell the roses in our front yard, eat fresh vegetables grown from tiny seeds we had selected, eat fruit from trees grown in our back yard. No longer were we able to reminisce about the days gone by, anticipate the future, or take turns spoiling the great grands. No more trips to South Africa or Singapore together; no longer could we travel back to upstate New York to visit the families we enabled to secure their first home. This indeed was the valley for me.

There is still one more ministry in which I spend a considerable amount of time; it is a ministry of helping other caregivers who are caring for love ones with dementia. It is called the *African American Alzheimer's Caregiver Training and Support Project.* The primary purpose of the project is to train African Americans who are caring for older adults with Alzheimer's how to take better care of themselves.

At my lowest point, one morning I received a telephone call from Flood Willis, M.D., Head of Family Medicine, Mayo Clinic, Jacksonville who gave me a number to call in the College of Medicine, Florida State University, Tallahassee, FL. On the other end of my phone call was Robert Glueckauf, Ph.D., Professor, Department of Behavioral Sciences & Social Medicine. After I listened to Dr. Glueckauf talk about the benefits of the African American Alzheimer's Caregivers Training and Support project (ACTS) for a few minutes, I asked, where can I go to participate in this program? I was advised that the training consisted of twelve weekly sessions conducted over the telephone. I questioned the effectiveness of any program done via phone. What I learned; the Florida State University College of Medicine and the Mayo Clinic- Jacksonville had conducted research to evaluate the effectiveness of face-to-face groups vs telephone groups. Their findings revealed, telephone groups were more effective for the following reasons: 1) caregivers did not have to dress and travel to the site of the meetings, 2) caregivers did not have to get someone to care for their love one with dementia while attending the meetings, 3) caregivers did not have to incur the expense of transportation and parking fees, and 4) participants in telephone based groups were significantly more likely to complete the training.

The program consists of twelve weekly sessions focusing on: Dementia 101, relaxation techniques, effective thinking, increasing emotional well-being, assertive responding, how to deal with challenging situations; and, five sessions of problem solving and, wrap-up and techniques for maintaining gains. I enrolled in the program and was significantly helped. I probably would not be telling this story had I not participated in the African American Alzheimer's Training and Support project.

Six months after completing the training, I was recruited as a facilitator. That is, I was asked to train other caregivers. I have successfully facilitated five different groups, made more than fifty presentations, participated in a PBS television documentary, served as a liaison volunteer and now serve as Chair of the Advisory Board.

This is a part of my ministry. I do not want to participate in another funeral where the caregiver dies before the care recipient. It is my goal and the goal of the project director that the African American Alzheimer's Training and Support Program become fully incorporated in the ministry of the African American churches as a vital part of a comprehensive health ministry. It is my belief that lay persons who are gifted, trained, nurtured, supported and held accountable can do many tasks now done by professionals. The health care professionals would play a major role to ensure: proper training of facilitators, rigid quality control, research and evaluation. This arrangement would employ another model of health care delivery, provide needed service to underserved populations in a manner that respects their dignity in their own communities. I thank God that he has allowed me to help guide this ministry in a new, innovative, direction.

We are making inroads in the African American Churches; African Methodist Episcopal, 11th Episcopal District, The Primitive Baptist State Convention have endorsed this ministry and invested financial resources. Some judicatories of the Missionary Baptist have recently joined forces. The incidence of Alzheimer's disease is expected to double in the Caucasian population within the next fifteen to twenty years. For the same period, it is expected to quadruple in the African American community. The literature suggests African Americans caring for love ones with dementia often do more of the heavy, demanding work, are more likely to neglect their own health and spend a higher percentage of their income on their love one (Caring for a person with Alzheimer's disease (The National Institute on Aging, Dec. 19, 2012). It is my desire that every African American church develop a comprehensive ministry to serve those persons in the community who are caring for love ones with dementia. I have traveled throughout the state of Florida, speaking in local African American congregations, conventions, conferences and associations advocating for those caring for love ones with dementia. We still have a long way to go to get buy-in, but we have made the first step.

CHAPTER 19

THE LAST MILES

———◆———

I began this book by identifying the physical place of my early childhood years. I labeled it as "over the river." As I look back on eighty-nine years of life "over the river" has taken on a new meaning- not physical but spiritual. "Over the river," for me, is more than a physical, geographical community, it is a psychological, spiritual community. "Over the river" means that by the grace of God, I have overcome. I have endured the bitter stings of segregation, the pain of seeing my father saying, "Yes sir" to young white boys, not much older than his son, Jim Crow, racism, inferior public schools, the struggles of getting an education.

Those destructive, dehumanizing, brutally painful experiences are a part of who I am. Those types experiences are not unique to me. They were every-day occurrences in the lives of many African Americans who live in this racist society. Bitter and painful as were those negative experiences, were overshadowed by two devoted, loving parents. They were parents who believed in God, believed in themselves and believed their children could climb any mountain and cross any sea. My parents instilled in me; you are no better than anyone else, but you are just as good. Therefore, I have never felt inferior. I have always believed I could go "over the river."

"Over the river" at this point in my life demonstrates that with determination, hard work, faith in God and a willingness to set goals and work to make them reality, one can achieve anything. At this point in life, James Weldon Johnson words in "Lift Every Voice and Sing" expresses my view of my present state:

Stony the road we trod, bitter the chastening rod,

felt in the days when Hope unborn had died;

yet with a steady beat, have not our weary feet

come to the place for which our fathers sighed?

We have come over a way that with tears have been watered,

we have come, treading our path through

the blood of the slaughtered;

out from the gloomy past,

till now we stand at last

where the white gleam of our bright star is cast

(AME Hymnal, 571).

By God's grace, I have received degrees from the following institutions of higher learning: Bachelor of Science, Florida Agricultural and Mechanical University, Tallahassee, Florida; Master of Divinity, Turner Theological Seminary in the Interdenominational

Theological Center, Atlanta, Georgia; Master of Social Work, State University of New York Buffalo, Buffalo, New York and Doctor of Ministry, Drew University, Madison, New Jersey. I have taught in the military, in the public schools of Suwannee and Palm Beach Counties, Florida and in the school of Social Work at Florida State University, Tallahassee, Florida. Moreover, I have served as college chaplain, Associate Eexecutive Director, New York State Council of Churches, Syracuse, New York; Veterans Administrator Chaplain, Batavia, New York; Administrator, Mental Health Services, Jordan Health Center, Rochester, New York; pastor and presiding elder in the Africa Methodist Episcopal Church.

"Over the river" means that I serve as a mentor for Master of Divinity and dissertation coach for a doctoral student at Asbury Theological Seminary, Orlando, Florida. In addition, I am a leader in the justice ministry, and chair the advisory Board of the African American Alzheimer's Caregivers Training and Support project at the College of Medicine, Florida State University, Tallahassee, Florida. I teach a Sunday school class and serve as a caregiver for my wife of 64 years. My journey has been one of ups and downs, falling and rising. It has also been marked with unimaginable accomplishments. The son of a sharecropper has risen to every position in the African Methodist Episcopal Church, except the office of bishop. I have served as pastor of Good Hope, Pensacola; Springfield, Gretna; Saint

Hebron, Quincy, Hurst Chapel, Winter Haven; and Saint Paul, Jacksonville, all in Florida.

This is my story. This is my "over the river."

POST SCRIPT

---◆---

In the presence of God and of Christ Jesus, who will judge the living and the dead, and because he is coming to rule as king, I solemnly urge ²you to preach the message, to insist upon proclaiming it (whether the time is right or not), to convince, reproach, and encourage, as you teach with all patience. ³The time will come when people will not listen to sound doctrine, but will follow their own desires and will collect for themselves more and more teachers who will tell them what they are itching to hear. ⁴They will turn away from listening to the truth and give their attention to legends. ⁵But you must keep control of yourself in all circumstances; endure suffering, do the work of a preacher of the Good News, and perform your whole duty as a servant of God. ⁶As for me, the hour has come for me to be sacrificed; the time is here for me to leave this life. ⁷have done my best in the race, I have run the full distance. ⁸And now there is waiting for me the victory prize of being put right with God, which the Lord, the righteous Judge, will give me on that Day- and not only to me, but to all those who wait with love for him to appear (2 Timothy 4:1-8 TEV).

"May the grace of the Lord Jesus Christ be with everyone."

James Melvin Proctor, D. Min.

ABOUT THE AUTHOR

———◆———

Dr. Proctor actively participates in the Christian education ministry at Greater Grant Memorial African Methodist Episcopal Church, teaching an adult church school class. He is a leader and strong advocate for Grant's justice ministry. He is chair of the Advisory Board, African American Alzheimer's Caregiver Training and Support project, College of Medicine, Florida State University, Tallahassee, FL

He received his Bachelors of Science degree from Florida A and M University, Tallahassee, FL; Master of Divinity at Turner Theological Seminary in the Interdenominational Theological Center, Atlanta, GA; Master of Social Work, State University of New York Buffalo, Buffalo, NY and the Doctor of Ministry at Drew University, Madison, NJ.

Dr. Proctor's career has been rich and varied. He has taught in high schools and at the university level. He served as an administrator of Mental Health at Jordan Health Center, Rochester, NY, associate executive director of the New York State Council of Churches, Syracuse, NY, community development worker, and itinerant elder and pastor in the African Methodist Episcopal church for more than fifty years. He is married to Rose Gallon Proctor. They have one adult son.